Illustrated English Idioms Book 2

Levels: B1 & B2

get our act together

go broke

be at his beck and call

caught him in the act

crocodile tears

bed of roses

cost an arm and a leg.

couch potato

hard cheese

rock the boat

Andrew Betsis
Lawrence Mamas

Illustrated Idioms

Preface

An idiom is an **expression**, a colloquial metaphor, which has a figurative meaning that is known only through common use. The meaning of this phrase or expression cannot be deduced by finding the meaning of each individual word.

Idioms are considered part of the language's culture and, in order to be understood, they require some knowledge, information, or experience that the members of this culture share. It is believed that William Shakespeare coined over 2,000 idioms that are still in use today.

Example: e.g. *If you finish your lessons, you can come with me;* **the ball's in your court** now.

In the English language expression: *the ball's in your court now*, a non-native speaker would be unable to deduce the actual meaning of this phrase, which has nothing to do with sports and it is used to show that somebody is responsible for the **next move in a situation**. Although it can refer literally to sports/football, it is rarely used in that way. Also, it cannot always be directly translated to other languages because it might have a completely different meaning. However, some idioms can be found in many different languages and they can be easily translated, or their metaphorical meaning can be easily deduced.

Idioms are very important in English and quite difficult for students to learn. Students have to learn idiomatic expressions the way they learn other vocabulary. Some of the most common ones that students will come across are dealt with in this book.

Some things to keep in mind about idioms are:
a) The meaning of an idiom cannot be deduced by a literal translation of its spare words.
b) We cannot substitute a word in an idiom with a word similar in meaning.
c) We cannot usually modify an idiomatic phrase syntactically.

This book aims to build up students' knowledge of Idioms through full-colour illustrations, which are accompanied by graded exercises. Throughout each unit, the new Idioms introduced are recycled, and students are exposed to every new Idiom on seven (7) different occasions.

There are also 2 Review Units (*Review Unit 1: Units 1-5* and *Review Unit 2: Units 6-10*), which also revise and consolidate the Idioms that students have already been taught.

The book is intended for intermediate/upper- intermediate level students (**B1** and **B2**), or even more advanced students (**IELTS** Score: *from 5.0 up to 7.0*) who want to practise or revise their knowledge of this area of the language. It can be used in the classroom, or for self-study purposes. The exercises can be given as homework and then discussed in class.

Published by
GLOBAL ELT LTD
www.globalelt.co.uk
Copyright © **GLOBAL ELT LTD 2013**
The right of Andrew Betsis and Lawrence Mamas to be identified as the authors of this work has been asserted in accordance with the Copyright, Designs and Patent Act 1988.

All rights reserved.
No part of this publication may be reproduced, stored in a retrieval system, or transmitted in any form or by any means, electronic, mechanical, photocopying, recording or otherwise, without the prior permission in writing of the Publisher.
Any person who does any unauthorised act in relation to this publication may be liable to criminal prosecution and civil claims for damages.

British Library Cataloguing-in-Publication Data
A catalogue record of this book is available from the British Library.

- ILLUSTRATED IDIOMS BOOK 2 Levels: B1 & B2 - TEACHER'S BOOK **ISBN:** 978-1-78164-099-9
- ILLUSTRATED IDIOMS BOOK 2 Levels: B1 & B2 - STUDENT'S BOOK **ISBN:** 978-1-78164-098-2

Contents

UNIT 1	Page 5
UNIT 2	Page 11
UNIT 3	Page 17
UNIT 4	Page 23
UNIT 5	Page 29
REVIEW UNIT: UNITS 1-5	Page 35
UNIT 6	Page 39
UNIT 7	Page 45
UNIT 8	Page 51
UNIT 9	Page 57
UNIT 10	Page 63
REVIEW UNIT: UNITS 6-10	Page 69
IDIOMS INDEX	Page 74
IRREGULAR VERBS INDEX	Page 76

Illustrated Idioms

The structure of each Unit:

The Idioms are presented with their definitions at the beginning of the unit.

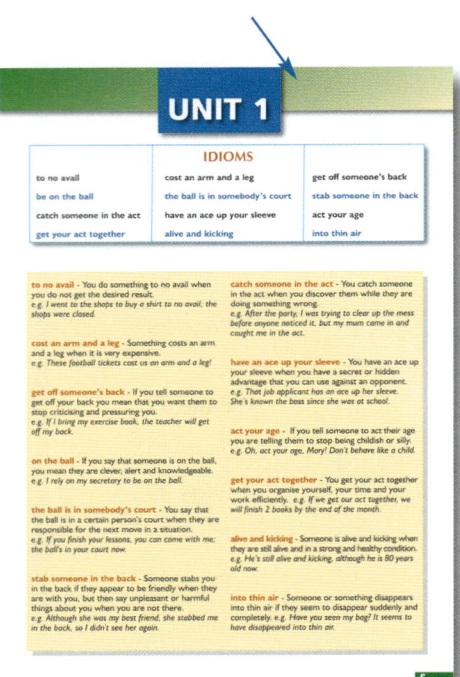

Full colour illustrations show what each Idiom means, accompanied by Activity A (matching/gap-filling).

A variety of Exercises help students master the use of the most frequent Idioms.

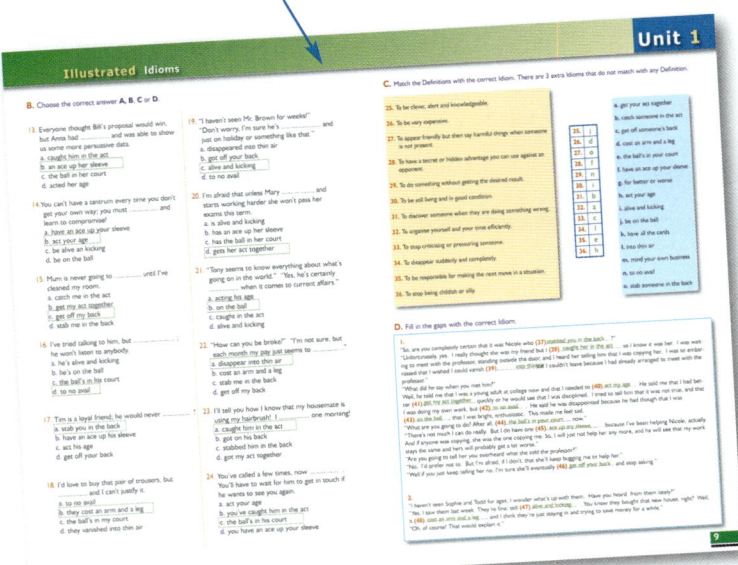

A fun activity for revising the Idioms is provided at the end of each unit.

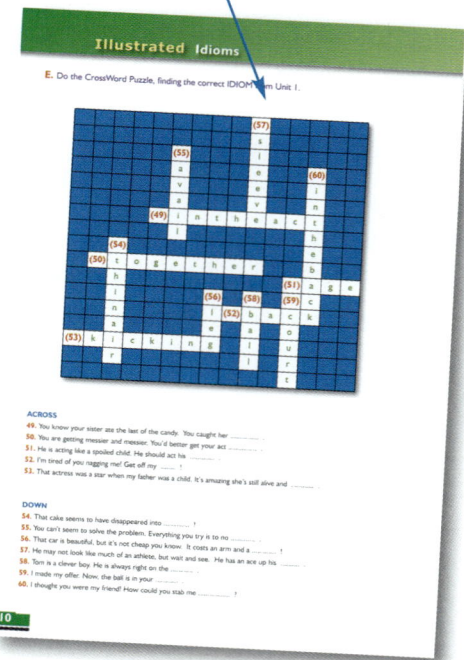

UNIT 1

IDIOMS

to no avail	cost an arm and a leg	get off someone's back
be on the ball	the ball is in somebody's court	stab someone in the back
catch someone in the act	have an ace up your sleeve	act your age
get your act together	(to be) alive and kicking	vanish/disappear into thin air

to no avail - You do something to no avail when you attempt it but do not get the desired result.
e.g. *I went to the shops to buy a shirt to no avail; the shops were closed.*

cost an arm and a leg - Something costs an arm and a leg when it is very expensive.
e.g. *These football tickets cost us an arm and a leg!*

get off someone's back - If you tell someone to get off your back you mean that you want them to stop criticising and pressuring you.
e.g. *If I bring my exercise book, the teacher will get off my back.*

on the ball - If you say that someone is on the ball, you mean they are clever and/or alert and/or knowledgeable.
e.g. *I rely on my secretary to be on the ball.*

the ball is in somebody's court - You say that the ball is in a certain person's court when he or she is responsible for the next move in a situation.
e.g. *If you finish your homework, you can come with me; the ball's in your court now.*

stab someone in the back - Someone stabs you in the back if they appear to be friendly when they are with you, but then say unpleasant or harmful things about you when you are not there.
e.g. *Although she was my best friend, she stabbed me in the back, so I never want to see her again.*

catch someone in the act - You catch someone in the act when you discover them while they are doing something wrong.
e.g. *After the party, I was trying to clear up the mess before anyone noticed it, but my mum came in and caught me in the act.*

have an ace up your sleeve - You have an ace up your sleeve when you have a secret or hidden advantage that you can use against an opponent.
e.g. *That job applicant has an ace up her sleeve. She's known the boss since she was at school.*

act your age - If you tell someone to act their age you are telling them to stop being childish or silly.
e.g. *Oh, act your age, Mary! Don't behave like a child.*

get your act together - You get your act together when you organise yourself, your time and/or your work efficiently.
e.g. *If we get our act together, we will finish 2 books by the end of the month.*

(to be) alive and kicking - Someone is alive and kicking when they are still alive and in a strong and healthy condition.
e.g. *He's still alive and kicking, although he is 80 years old now.*

vanish / disappear into thin air - Someone or something disappears into thin air if it/they seem to disappear suddenly and completely. e.g. *Have you seen my bag? It seems to have disappeared into thin air.*

Illustrated Idioms

A. Fill in the gaps in the sentences below with the correct Idiom from Unit 1.

1. I can't believe these shoes have broken already; they .... !

4. I have scoured books and magazines for any information on this subject, but so far ....

2. I wouldn't have hired my brother if he wasn't completely ....

5. If I could just pay this last instalment, the bank manager might finally ....

3. Bob knew his colleague would take any opportunity to ...., so he was careful to watch what he said.

6. I told them we were interested in buying, but at a lower price; so .... now.

Unit 1

7. I bet he's got .... ; he wouldn't let anybody beat him that easily.

8. We're going to have to .... if we want to finish this job by the end of the week.

9. My keys seem to have ....

10. The robber was trying to escape with the money, but I .... !

11. Why don't you put those computer games away and .... for once?

12. No, he's not dead! He's ...., and from what I hear, still going to the gym regularly.

Illustrated Idioms

B. Choose the correct answer A, B, C or D.

13. Everyone thought Bill's proposal would win, but Anna had .... and was able to show us some more persuasive data.
    a. caught him in the act
    b. an ace up her sleeve
    c. the ball in her court
    d. acted her age

14. You can't have a tantrum every time you don't get your own way; you must .... and learn to compromise!
    a. have an ace up your sleeve
    b. act your age
    c. be alive and kicking
    d. be on the ball

15. Mum is never going to .... until I've cleaned my room.
    a. catch me in the act
    b. get my act together
    c. get off my back
    d. stab me in the back

16. I've tried talking to him, but .... ; he won't listen to anybody.
    a. he's alive and kicking
    b. he's on the ball
    c. the ball's in his court
    d. to no avail

17. Tim is a loyal friend; he would never .... !
    a. stab you in the back
    b. have an ace up his sleeve
    c. act his age
    d. get off your back

18. I'd love to buy that pair of trousers, but .... and I can't justify it.
    a. to no avail
    b. they cost an arm and a leg
    c. the ball's in my court
    d. they vanished into thin air

19. "I haven't seen Mr. Brown for weeks!" "Don't worry, I'm sure he's .... and just on holiday or something like that."
    a. disappeared into thin air
    b. got off your back
    c. alive and kicking
    d. to no avail

20. I'm afraid that unless Mary .... and starts working harder she won't pass her exams this term.
    a. is alive and kicking
    b. disappears into thin air
    c. has the ball in her court
    d. gets her act together

21. "Tony seems to know everything about what's going on in the world." "Yes, he's certainly .... when it comes to current affairs."
    a. acting his age
    b. on the ball
    c. caught in the act
    d. getting off your back

22. A: "How can you be broke?" B: "I'm not sure, but each month my pay just seems to ...."
    a. disappear into thin air
    b. cost an arm and a leg
    c. stab me in the back
    d. get off my back

23. I'll tell you how I know that my housemate is using my hairbrush! I .... one morning!
    a. caught him in the act
    b. got on his back
    c. stabbed him in the back
    d. got my act together

24. You've called a few times, now .... You'll have to wait for him to get in touch if he wants to see you again.
    a. act your age
    b. you've caught him in the act
    c. the ball's in his court
    d. you have an ace up your sleeve

8

Unit 1

C. Match the Definitions with the correct Idiom. There are 3 extra Idioms that do not match with any Definition.

25. To be clever, alert and knowledgeable.

26. To be very expensive.

27. To appear friendly but then say harmful things when someone is not present.

28. To have a secret or hidden advantage you can use against an opponent.

29. To do something without getting the desired result.

30. To be still living and in good condition.

31. To discover someone when they are doing something wrong.

32. To organise yourself and/or your time efficiently.

33. To stop criticising or pressuring someone.

34. To disappear suddenly and completely.

35. To be responsible for making the next move in a situation.

36. To stop being childish or silly.

25.	
26.	
27.	
28.	
29.	
30.	
31.	
32.	
33.	
34.	
35.	
36.	

a. get your act together
b. catch someone in the act
c. get off someone's back
d. cost an arm and a leg
e. the ball's in your court
f. have an ace up your sleeve
g. for better or worse
h. act your age
i. alive and kicking
j. be on the ball
k. have all the cards
l. vanish into thin air
m. mind your own business
n. to no avail
o. stab someone in the back

D. Fill in the gaps with the correct Idiom.

1.
A: "So, are you completely certain that it was Nicole who (37).......................... ?"
B: "Unfortunately, yes. I really thought she was my friend but I (38).......................... so I know it was her. I was waiting to meet with the professor, standing outside the door, and I heard her telling him that I was copying her. I was so embarrassed that I wished I could (39).......................... , but I couldn't leave because I had already arranged to meet with the professor."
A: "What did he say when you met him?"
B: "Well, he told me that I was a young adult at college now and that I needed to (40).................... . He told me that I had better (41).......................... quickly or he would see that I was disciplined. I tried to tell him that it was not true, and that I was doing my own work, but (42).................... . He said he was disappointed because he had thought that I was (43)....................; that I was bright and enthusiastic. This made me feel sad."
A: "What are you going to do? After all, (44).......................... now."
B: "There's not much I can do really. But I do have one (45).......................... , because I've been helping Nicole, actually. And if anyone was copying, she was the one copying me. So, I will just not help her anymore, and he will see that my work stays the same and hers will probably get a lot worse."
A: "Are you going to tell her you overheard what she told the professor?"
B: "No. I'd prefer not to. But I'm afraid, if I don't, that she'll keep bugging me to help her."
A: "Well if you just keep telling her no, I'm sure she'll eventually (46).......................... and stop asking."

2.
A: "I haven't seen Sophie and Todd for ages; I wonder what's up with them. Have you heard from them lately?"
B: "Yes, I saw them last week. They're fine; still (47).......................... . You know they bought that new house, right? Well, it (48).......................... and I think they're just staying in and trying to save money for a while."
A: "Oh, of course! That would explain it."

9

Illustrated Idioms

E. Do the CrossWord Puzzle, finding the correct IDIOM from Unit 1.

ACROSS

49. You know your sister ate the last of the candy. You caught her ....
50. You are getting messier and messier. You'd better get your act ....
51. He is acting like a spoiled child. He should act his ....
52. I'm tired of you nagging me! Get off my .... !
53. That actress was a star when my father was a child. It's amazing she's still alive and ....

DOWN

54. That cake seems to have disappeared into .... !
55. You can't seem to solve the problem. Everything you try is to no ....
56. That car is beautiful, but it's not cheap you know. It costs an arm and a .... !
57. He may not look like much of an athlete, but wait and see. He has an ace up his ....
58. Tom is a clever boy. He is always right on the ....
59. I have made my offer. Now, the ball is in your ....
60. I thought you were my friend! How could you stab me .... ?

10

UNIT 2

IDIOMS

(to be) no bed of roses	(to be) at someone's beck and call	(to have) a bee in your bonnet
get out of bed on the wrong side	(to have) beginner's luck	beggars can't be choosers
(to be) saved by the bell	rings a bell	better late than never
give the benefit of the doubt	(to be) below the belt	better safe than sorry

(to be) no bed of roses - If you tell someone that something is no bed of roses, or not a bed of roses, you mean that it's difficult or not always pleasant.
e.g. *It's no bed of roses working as a miner.*

(to be) at someone's beck and call - You are at someone's beck and call if you are always ready to carry out their orders or wishes.
e.g. *"Bring me my slippers!" "Get them yourself! I'm not at your beck and call, you know.*

(to have) a bee in your bonnet - You have a bee in your bonnet when you have an idea or belief that has become an obsession. e.g. *"Is she still worrying about my diet?" "You know her - once she gets a bee in her bonnet she won't let the matter rest."*

get out of bed on the wrong side - You say that you have got out of bed on the wrong side when little things keep going wrong for you; you can also say that someone got out of bed on the wrong side when they seem to be in a bad mood.
e.g. *What's the matter with Alan today? Did he get out of bed on the wrong side?*

(to have) beginner's luck - You have beginner's luck when you are unexpectedly successful at an early stage of learning something.
e.g. *Congratulations to your new Assistant Editor, who (thanks to a large slice of beginner's luck!) made accurate predictions for all the World Cup matches.*

beggars can't be choosers - If you say that beggars can't be choosers, you mean that people who have a great need for something have to accept whatever is offered. e.g. *I don't want to live with my parents; I want to have my own house but beggars can't be choosers, I suppose.*

(to be) saved by the bell - People sometimes exclaim "saved by the bell!" when someone is rescued from an unpleasant or difficult situation by something which brings the situation to an abrupt or sudden end.
e.g. *Luckily I was saved by the bell when the movie started; I didn't have to tell Mr. Jones that I thought what he was saying was nonsense!*

rings a bell - Something such as a name rings a bell if it is familiar or reminds you of something.
e.g. *The title of the book rang a bell but I couldn't remember if I had read it.*

give someone the benefit of the doubt - You give someone the benefit of the doubt when you accept that what they say is true, even though there is no evidence to support it. e.g. *I don't know if you're telling me the truth but I'll give you the benefit of the doubt.*

(to be) below the belt - A remark or comment that is below the belt is unkind and unfair, or unacceptable.
e.g. *"Perhaps, Mr Prentice, as you're obviously out of work, you should now take a course in housekeeping." That was below the belt, but she went on.*

better late than never - You say "better late than never" either to show someone that you are not very pleased that they are late, or if you think that it is preferable that something should happen late, rather than not at all.
e.g. *You will have to accept that some permanent damage may already have occurred. Better to get treatment late than never, though.*

better safe than sorry - You say "better safe than sorry" when you want to remind someone that it's worth taking precautions, or to tell them not to be afraid of raising the alarm if they see something suspicious.
e.g. *If you see someone acting suspiciously near your house, call the police. Don't worry if it turns out to be a false alarm; it's always better to be safe than sorry.*

Illustrated Idioms

A. Fill in the gaps in the sentences below with the correct Idiom from Unit 2.

1. I had to be .... night and day, and he would often get me out of bed late at night to run an errand.

2. I must've .... today – that's the second cup of coffee I've spilt.

3. I didn't really want to take a job like this again but, since I'm unemployed, I suppose ....

4. It's .... teaching in a secondary school.

5. Billy has got .... about reaching those apples, hasn't he! He's been out there for an hour already!

6. When I won the first time I played, I put it down to ....

Unit 2

7. Her name .... ; she's named after a flower; I think Margarita is the Greek word for a daisy.

10. Toby hated swimming lessons, but was .... when the swimming instructor had to leave in a hurry.

8. John knew that his brother had a secret, so when he used it against him, it was like hitting him ....

11. "I'll give you .... this time, but you must bring your identification with you next time."

9. You might as well take out holiday insurance even though your not doing anything dangerous; .... !

12. "Michael! You're a whole hour late coming in to the office! Still, ... I suppose."

Illustrated Idioms

B. Choose the correct answer A, B, C or D.

13. Don't .... about working out; there is such a thing as too much exercise you know!
    a. get out of bed on the wrong side
    b. ring a bell
    c. get a bee in your bonnet
    d. be saved by the bell

14. You should get health insurance even if you're healthy; it's always ....
    a. better late than never.
    b. better to be safe than sorry.
    c. the benefit of the doubt.
    d. beginner's luck.

15. I'm enjoying university life, but it's certainly .... ; we have to study very hard.
    a. no bed of roses
    b. beginner's luck
    c. better late than never
    d. below the belt

16. That was .... ; telling Amy that she's fat! You know how sensitive she is about her weight.
    a. beginner's luck
    b. better safe than sorry
    c. ringing a bell
    d. below the belt

17. You must have .... today, because you are annoyed by everything I say!
    a. beginner's luck
    b. a bee in your bonnet
    c. got out of bed on the wrong side
    d. the benefit of the doubt

18. She was told to stay a few hours longer, but .... when I arrived to do her shift.
    a. was saved by the bell
    b. was given the benefit of the doubt
    c. got out of bed on the wrong side
    d. it's better late than never

19. She is spoiling that child! She's .... all the time and does whatever he wants.
    a. saved by the bell
    b. got a bee in her bonnet
    c. better safe than sorry
    d. at his beck and call

20. Sandwiches are not my favourite food but it was free, after all, so ....
    a. better safe than sorry
    b. beggars can't be choosers
    c. better late than never
    d. it was no bed of roses

21. "I can't believe you just hit the bull's eye four times!"
    "It's my first game of darts so it must .... !"
    a. be beginner's luck
    b. be a bed of roses
    c. be below the belt
    d. ring a bell

22. Something about his face ....
    a. is at my beck and call
    b. gives me the benefit of the doubt
    c. is below the belt
    d. rings a bell

23. You should .... unless, of course, you have proof that she stole it.
    a. ring a bell
    b. be at her beck and call
    c. get a bee in your bonnet
    d. give her the benefit of the doubt

24. At the age of 65, you will be older than most undergraduates, but .... !
    a. beggars can't be choosers
    b. better late than never
    c. it's no bed of roses
    d. better safe than sorry

Unit 2

C. Match the Definitions with the correct Idiom. There are 3 extra Idioms that do not match with any Definition.

25. Something unpleasant or difficult.

26. Always waiting to carry out someone's orders.

27. An idea or belief that becomes an obsession.

28. To be in a bad mood or have things keep going wrong.

29. To be unexpectedly successful when you first learn something.

30. When someone needs something and accepts whatever is offered, what do we say?

31. Rescued from an unpleasant or difficult situation when it is suddenly interrupted.

32. When something seems familiar.

33. To believe that someone is not guilty because there is no proof.

34. When a remark is unkind, or unacceptable.

35. A statement of either displeasure or approval when someone does something later than expected.

36. We say this to remind someone to take precautions or be cautious.

a. saved by the bell
b. better late than never
c. a bee in your bonnet
d. alive and kicking
e. the ball's in your court
f. at someone's beck and call
g. get out of bed on the wrong side
h. to have beginner's luck
i. beggars can't be choosers
j. rings a bell
k. better safe than sorry
l. no bed of roses
m. below the belt
n. to no avail
o. give someone the benefit of the doubt

25.	
26.	
27.	
28.	
29.	
30.	
31.	
32.	
33.	
34.	
35.	
36.	

D. Fill in the gaps with the correct Idiom.

1.
My first day working as a nurse was quite a day! I would have preferred not to work at a big city hospital, but in these times I feel lucky just to have a job, and **(37)**................................. , after all. The hospital was very big and hectic and confusing. The doctor I work for seemed like he had **(38)**... because he was quite cross, or perhaps he had been there all night working, who knows. Anyway, he had **(39)**................................. about bedside manner, and must have told me about 12 times that day that it was my job to be **(40)**................................. of the patients. He said that it was **(41)**.............................. to be a patient in the hospital, and that if anyone ever complained of feeling unwell I must **(42)**... and take it seriously even if they seemed to be doing well because it's always **(43)**................................. . He also said that patients were often rude and difficult, and when I said that they all seemed nice enough to me so far, he said "**(44)**........................... !" I thought he was about to say something else negative, but I was **(45)**.............................. when his mobile phone rang and he rushed off.

2.
A: "Oh, hello. Do I know you? Your face **(46)**....................... but I can't work out where I've seen you before. Oh.... yes. You're the man who used to work with us ages ago, aren't you?"

B: "Sorry, Mr. Royston, but I think that's quite **(47)**........................... and unfair. I was only away on sick leave for a week, and I couldn't help catching the flu! I didn't do it on purpose! Now, if you will excuse me, I'm going to finish the Smith report."

A: "Well, it's **(48)**................................., I suppose ..."

Illustrated Idioms

E. Do the CrossWord Puzzle, finding the correct IDIOM from Unit 2.

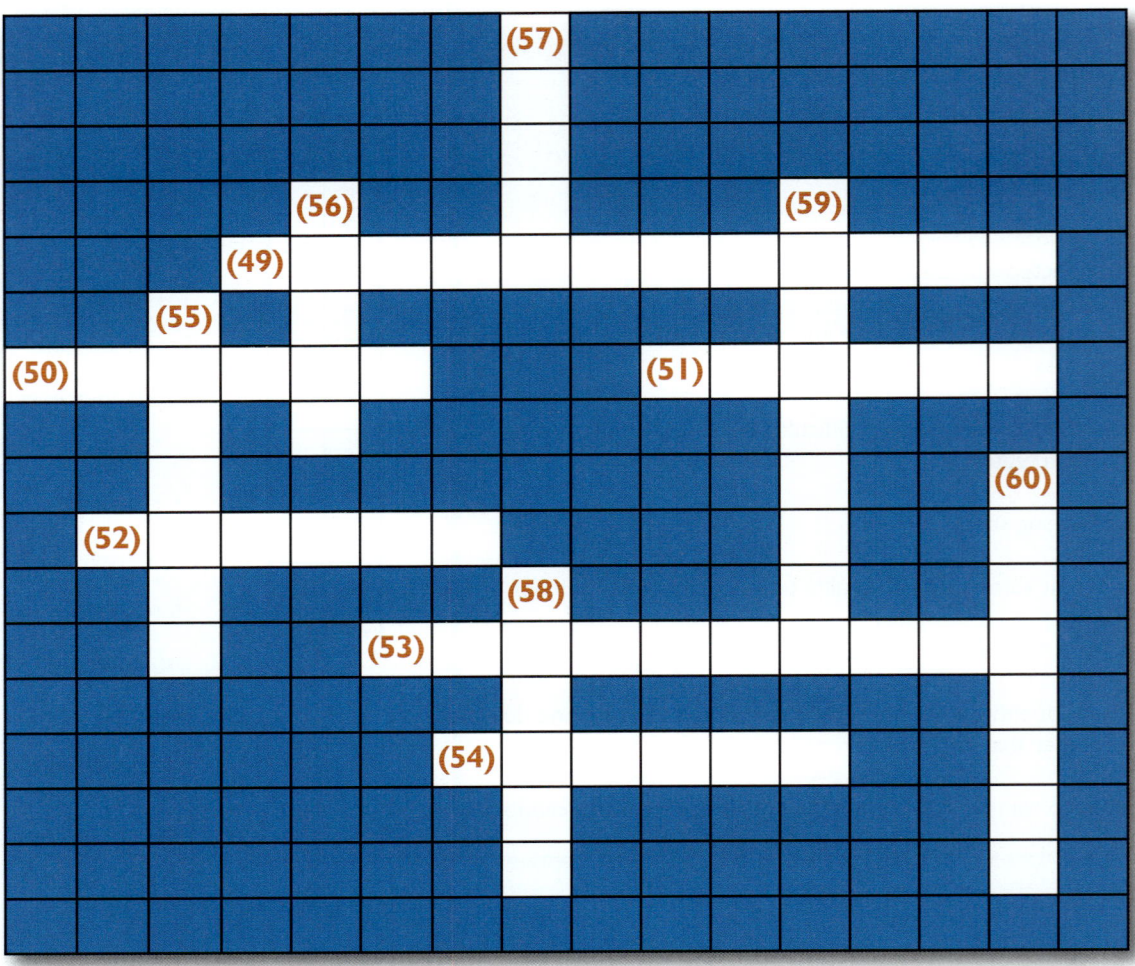

ACROSS
49. The secretary was always at her boss's ....
50. Your name seems familiar, but your face doesn't ring ....
51. I can't prove my innocence, but please give me the benefit of the ....
52. "Sorry I'm late." "Well, better late than ...."
53. "What's wrong with you?" "I must have got out of bed on the .... today."
54. I may seem cautious, but I always think it's better to be safe than ....

DOWN
55. Tim thinks we should save energy, but he has a bit of a bee in his .... and that's all I ever hear about.
56. That was below the .... to bring up his family problems at work!
57. Don't get over-confident, because it might only be beginner's .... !
58. Being an actor is not just a bed of .... ; it's a lot of hard work too.
59. I don't really like this apartment, but I thought I wasn't going to be able to find one, so beggars can't be ....
60. You've been saved by .... ! Stop studying now, we're going for lunch.

UNIT 3

IDIOMS

in the blink of an eye	a blessing in disguise	rock the boat
get the blues	cook the books	by the book
a bird in the hand is worth two in the bush	for better or worse	kill two birds with one stone
early bird	once bitten, twice shy	bits and pieces

in the blink of an eye - Something happens in the blink of an eye when it happens very quickly.
e.g. *The weather here is changeable; it can go from sun to hail in the blink of an eye!*

a blessing in disguise - Something is a blessing in disguise when it turns out to be the best thing that could have happened, despite seeming like a disaster at first.
e.g. *"The accident was probably a blessing in disguise," admits Barbara. "Otherwise I'd never have had time to start playing the piano."*

rock the boat - Someone rocks the boat when they disturb the balance or calmness of a situation, or cause trouble.
e.g. *Amazingly, our aunties are all getting along today, so don't rock the boat by bringing up something controversial!*

get the blues - You say that you've got the blues if you are feeling sad or depressed.
e.g. *Ever since we've moved to the city, I seem to get the blues almost every day.*

cook the books - Someone cooks the books when they change the numbers in their (or their company's) accounts illegally in order to save/make money.
e.g. *If you really believe that Zach is cooking the books, you should tell your boss right away!*

by the book - You do something by the book when you do it exactly according to the rules, or in the way you are supposed to do it.
e.g. *If you don't learn that computer programme by the book you could end up with some bad habits that will cost you a lot of time.*

a bird in the hand is worth two in the bush - People use "a bird in the hand is worth two in the bush", or just "a bird in the hand", to say it might not be worth giving up something you already have for only the possibility of something better.
e.g. *That job offer does sound good, but make sure you find out enough about it before you accept; after all, you're happy where you are now! You know, a bird in the hand...*

for better or worse - Something that is for better or worse will remain the same no matter what happens, good or bad.
e.g. *Our lives will change, for better or worse, now that oil is becoming scarce.*

kill two birds with one stone - You kill two birds with one stone when you manage to achieve two things with a single action.
e.g. *If you're going into town for shopping you might as well kill two birds with one stone and drop off the car for a tune up while you're there.*

early bird - An early bird is a person who gains some advantage by being early.
e.g. *If you're an early bird, and do your shopping before most people get out, you won't have to wait in line.*

once bitten, twice shy - A person who is once bitten, twice shy is afraid to try something again because of a previous bad experience.
e.g. *James fell off a horse when he was seven, and now he refuses to ride! Once bitten, twice shy, I guess.*

bits and pieces - Bits and pieces, are small things of various kinds. e.g. *I'm going to the corner shop for some bits and pieces; need anything?*

Illustrated Idioms

A. Fill in the gaps in the sentences below with the correct Idiom from Unit 3.

1. Being trapped in the cave turned into a .... when they found the ancient statue.

2. Whenever I .... I take a long walk in the hills or go for a bike ride.

3. They make us do everything ...., which doesn't give us much space for creativity.

4. She's good at spending a long time doing nothing, then becoming highly active ....

5. There is a risk that he may .... with his neighbours by playing his music so loud this late at night.

6. They are now saying that everyone is .... If it's true, it's a very serious allegation.

18

Unit 3

7. For .... , the computer has taken control of our lives.

10. You know how hard it is to catch birds! That's why they say ....

8. If you're an .... you'll be able to see the sunrise from the top of the mountain.

11. He tried to ....; first, he went out with his friends, and then he was back on time to watch TV.

9. Bill had to call a repairman after he tried to fix his car but then forgot how to put the .... back together.

12. He hasn't had a girlfriend now for two years; I think it's a case of ....

Illustrated Idioms

B. Choose the correct answer **A**, **B**, **C** or **D**.

13. There are advantages to an apprenticeship. You might as well .... by doing and learning in parallel.
    a. rock the boat
    b. cook the books
    c. kill two birds with one stone
    d. have a blessing in disguise

14. A few .... of yours are still here; would you like me to send them on to you?
    a. early birds
    b. blessings in disguise
    c. blinks of an eye
    d. bits and pieces

15. Michael is clever enough to .... and make a fortune, but he's honest; he'd never do it.
    a. cook the books
    b. rock the boat
    c. kill two birds with one stone
    d. go by the book

16. This is no time to act like .... ; we have every reason to celebrate!
    a. an early bird
    b. you've got the blues
    c. a blessing in disguise
    d. you've killed two birds with one stone

17. She says she's .... and will never marry again.
    a. rocked the boat
    b. going by the book
    c. once bitten, twice shy
    d. for better or worse

18. When he lost his job it was .... ; he went back to school, and then got a better one.
    a. a blessing in disguise
    b. a bird in the hand
    c. for better or worse
    d. once bitten, twice shy

19. You don't have to do everything ...., you know; sometimes it's better to try something different.
    a. for better or worse
    b. in the blink of an eye
    c. by the book
    d. to rock the boat

20. Are you sure a big house in the suburbs would really improve your life? You know, what they say: ....
    a. for better or worse
    b. once bitten, twice shy
    c. in the blink of an eye
    d. a bird in the hand is worth two in the bush

21. I know you don't want to .... and risk a fight, but I think you really must confront her!
    a. go by the book
    b. get the blues
    c. cook the books
    d. rock the boat

22. Six months may seem like a long time but it will pass ....
    a. for better or worse
    b. in bits and pieces
    c. in the blink of an eye
    d. by the book

23. She got the best seats in the theatre because she was .... and got there half an hour before the show started.
    a. a blessing in disguise
    b. an early bird
    c. by the book
    d. a bird in the hand

24. .... , he will have to take the bus to work now. His car is broken down.
    a. Once bitten, twice shy
    b. For better or worse
    c. By the book
    d. In the blink of an eye

Unit 3

C. Match the Definitions with the correct IDIOM. There are 3 extra Idioms that do not match with any Definition.

25. When something happens very quickly.

26. When something seems like a disaster at first, but turns out to be the best thing that could happen.

27. To disturb the balance of a situation or cause trouble.

28. To feel sad or depressed.

29. To change the numbers in an account in order to gain money.

30. Exactly according to the rules.

31. When it is not worth giving something up for the possibility of something better.

32. When something is as it is, no matter what is thought about it or what happens

33. To achieve two things with a single action.

34. Someone who gains some advantage by being early.

35. To be afraid of trying something because of a previous bad experience.

36. Small things, of various kinds.

a. kill two birds with one stone
b. costs an arm and a leg
c. in the blink of an eye
d. a bird in the hand
e. once bitten, twice shy
f. for better or worse
g. get the blues
h. rock the boat
i. by the book
j. rings a bell
k. bits and pieces
l. (an) early bird
m. cook the books
n. saved by the bell
o. a blessing in disguise

25.	
26.	
27.	
28.	
29.	
30.	
31.	
32.	
33.	
34.	
35.	
36.	

D. Fill in the gaps with the correct Idiom.

A: "What's wrong? You look like you've (37)........................ ."

B: "I do. Unfortunately, I've made a really bad decision. You see, I wanted to start a business of my own, and my cousin needed money, so I thought I could (38).................................. and buy his seafront cafe. It has a perfect location, particularly for the (39)..................... , because you can see the sun rise. But I didn't do things (40)....................... because I trusted him; he is family, after all! We agreed on a price and I bought it (41).................................. . I didn't take the time to check anything out, and now it's mine, (42)................................... ."

A: "But what's the matter? It sounds lovely!"

B: You're not going to believe this, but, actually, my cousin had been (43)................................ for many years, and the accounts are an absolute mess. Everything looked good on paper, but in reality there are big problems, and I don't know what to do, or even how serious the problems actually are!"

A: "Uh oh. Why don't you confront him?"

B: "I can't do that! It would cause big problems in my family, and I don't want to (44)......................... . I'll never trust him again though; (45)........................ as they say. I wish I'd left my money in the bank."

A: "It's true; (46)... ."

B: "But what can I do now? I just keep hoping it might turn into a (47).................................. . You never know how things might develop, after I've sorted out all the (48)............................... of paperwork that are a mess right now. After all, I am at least learning a lot from the experience!"

Illustrated Idioms

E. Do the CrossWord Puzzle, finding the correct IDIOM from Unit 3.

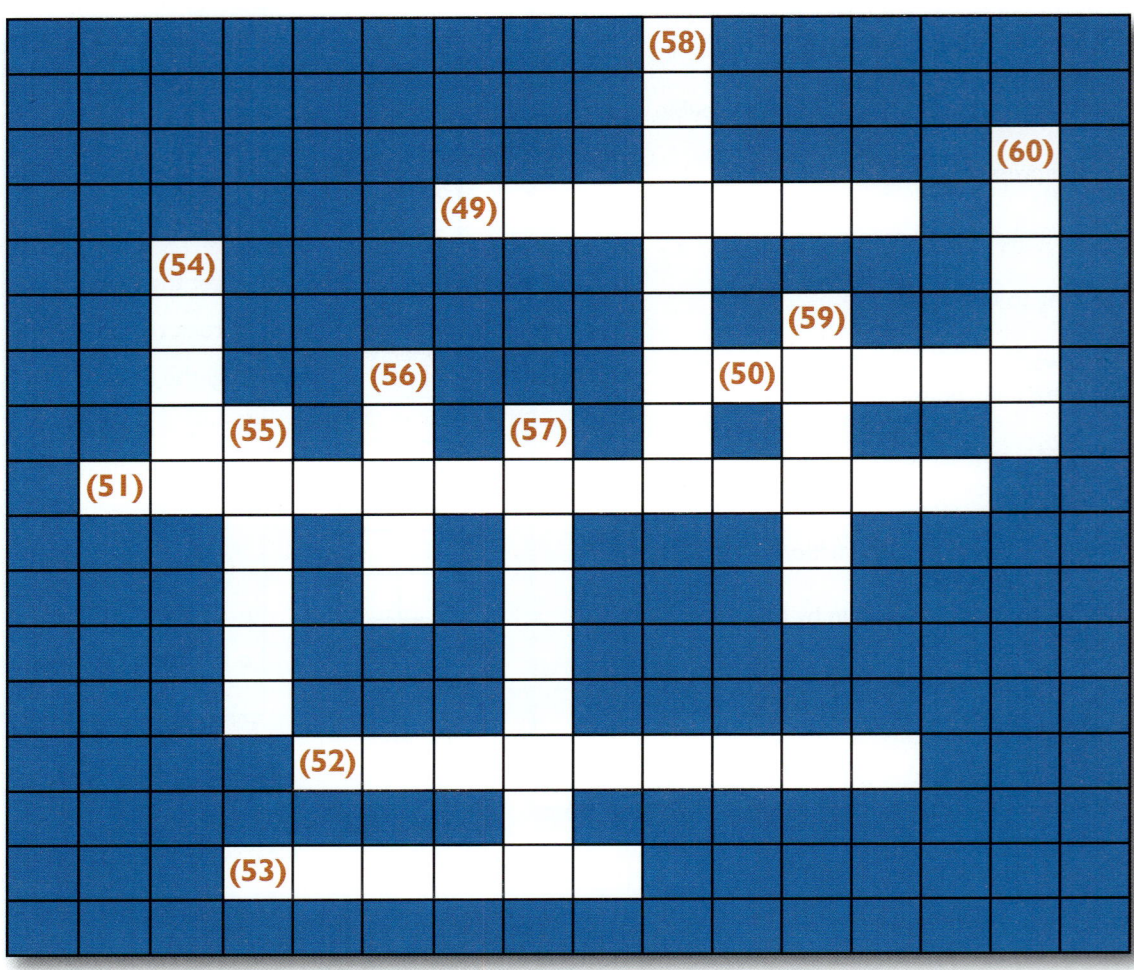

ACROSS

49. We have just a few bits and .... of furniture left to buy.

50. Johnny is kind of a rebel; he never does anything by the ....

51. I wouldn't take the chance; after all a bird in the hand is worth ....

52. I was stuck on a train for 12 hours once, but that was when I met my lovely husband, so I think it was a blessing in .... !"

53. It will be Christmas in the blink of ....

DOWN

54. If you're happy with the situation overall, then I wouldn't rock the ....

55. Times are changing, for better or ....

56. You need to be an early .... and leave before 8am to avoid traffic.

57. When it comes to taking financial risks, Bill lost out before, so it's a case of once bitten, ...

58. If you walk to work for exercise you will also save money, and so kill two birds with ....

59. I don't know why but I've got the .... today .

60. You'll get in lots of trouble if you're caught cooking the .... !

UNIT 4

IDIOMS

catch your breath	a breath of fresh air	kick the bucket
go broke	funny business	beat about/around the bush
know no bounds	from the bottom of your heart	out of bounds
get to the bottom of	give me a break	break even

catch your breath - You catch your breath when you stop breathing for a moment, because of fear, amazement or pain. *e.g. She caught her breath in pain when she shut her finger in the door.*

You catch your breath when you briefly stop doing (take a rest from) a physical activity in order to recover / regain lost energy / recuperate. *e.g. We stopped to catch our breath halfway up the mountain.*

a breath of fresh air - You describe someone or something as a breath of fresh air if you feel that they (or it) have (has) a fresh and positive influence on you and people in general. *e.g. Jenny's bubbly personality is a breath of fresh air wherever she goes.*

kick the bucket - Someone kicks the bucket when they die.
e.g. Don't give up; you're too young to kick the bucket!

go broke - A person or company goes broke when they lose all their money and cannot continue to work or trade properly. *e.g. Many people are going broke and losing their houses these days.*

funny business - Funny business consists of tricks or dishonest behaviour. *e.g. I don't trust them at all; I think there's some funny business going on.*

beat about/around the bush - You tell someone not to beat about/around the bush when you want them to speak openly and directly without delay and without hiding anything.
e.g. Speak your mind; don't beat around the bush!

know no bounds - Something which knows no bounds seems to be limitless.
e.g. Their selfishness seems to know no bounds!

from the bottom of your heart - You feel something from the bottom of your heart if you feel it very deeply and sincerely.
e.g. I respect him from the bottom of my heart.

out of bounds - A place is out of bounds when people or things are not allowed to go there.
e.g. Her team was upset with her for kicking the ball out of bounds.

get to the bottom of - You get to the bottom of a mystery, for example, when you find out its cause or when you solve it. *e.g. I'll talk to the member of staff concerned and get to the bottom of this.*

give me a break - You say to someone "Give me a break!" if you want them to stop annoying you. *e.g. You say I'm too slow? Give me a break! I'd like to see you do it faster!*

break even - A business breaks even when it makes as much money as it spends, but does not make a profit.
e.g. Breaking even is good, but it's not good enough! We need to make a profit too.

Illustrated Idioms

A. Fill in the gaps in the sentences below with the correct Idiom from Unit 4.

1. They remember him as a .... ; a manager who rejuvenated the team with his ability to motivate players.

4. A sudden noise made her ...., but it was only the wind.

2. After the factory closed, the residents of the town quickly began to ....

5. Honestly, I was so ill that I thought I was going to ....

3. You're a very clever child, making idiom jokes like this, but stop .... and tell me where my keys are!

6. Shelly gave me the money, but I think there was some .... because there was less than I expected.

Unit 4

7. She was touched .... when he gave her the flowers.

10. The generosity of the doctors involved in this charity ....

8. George finally .... the mystery of who (or what!) was nibbling on his food.

11. Shane always hits the ball .... on this part of the golf course.

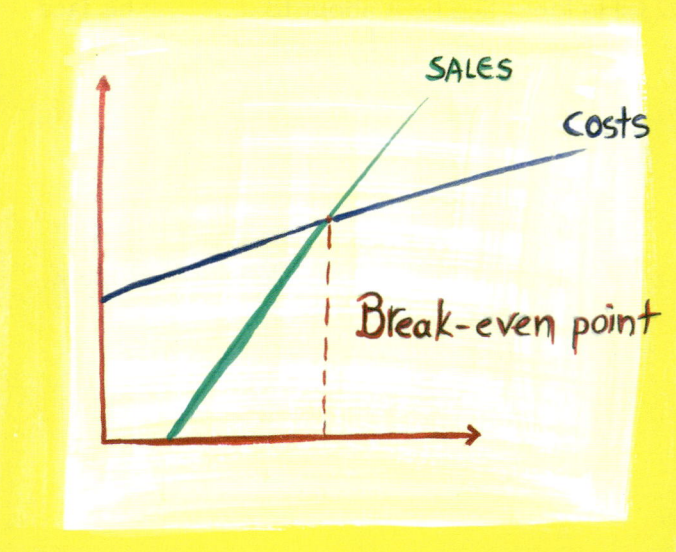

9. As you can see, in order to .... , our sales must increase as production costs increase.

12. .... ! We've been playing for only five minutes; you can't be tired already!

25

Illustrated Idioms

B. Choose the correct answer **A, B, C** or **D**.

13. Don't .... ; what exactly are you trying to say?
    a. kick the bucket
    b. beat around the bush
    c. break even
    d. get to the bottom of it

14. "Haven't you finished yet?"   "Oh, just .... , will you? I'll do it in my own time.
    a. catch your breath
    b. give me a break
    c. kick the bucket
    d. go broke

15. We would like to thank you ....
    a. like a breath of fresh air
    b. out of bounds
    c. from the bottom of our hearts
    d. for beating around the bush

16. The playing fields .... to pupils during the lunch break.
    a. are out of bounds
    b. are funny business
    c. are a breath of fresh air
    d. know no bounds

17. Although we .... at the end of the year, we were unable to go on paying the staff's wages.
    a. went broke
    b. kicked the bucket
    c. caught our breath
    d. broke even

18. He will do anything for money; his greed seems to ....
    a. break even
    b. go broke
    c. know no bounds
    d. kick the bucket

19. I don't think it's a wise move to get involved in ....
    a. a breath of fresh air
    b. breaking even
    c. the bottom of your heart
    d. funny business

20. If you really need an answer, Inspector Smith will ....
    a. know no bounds
    b. beat around the bush
    c. give you a break
    d. get to the bottom of it

21. Let's take a moment to .... before we climb higher.
    a. give me a break
    b. catch our breath
    c. kick the bucket
    d. beat around the bush

22. The new professor brought a much needed .... to the history department.
    a. breath of fresh air
    b. funny business
    c. from the bottom of his heart
    d. out of bounds

23. He looks like he is about to .... ; his face has no colour whatsoever!
    a. kick the bucket
    b. break even
    c. give me a break
    d. know no bounds

24. If you .... you can file for bankruptcy.
    a. break even
    b. go broke
    c. know no bounds
    d. kick the bucket

Unit 4

C. Match the Definitions with the correct Idioms. There are 3 extra Idioms that do not match with any Definition.

25. To stop breathing for a moment because of fear, amazement or pain / or to take a short rest after exerting yourself.

26. Someone who brings a positive influence.

27. To die.

28. Lose all your money.

29. Tricks and dishonest behaviour.

30. To not speak your mind openly or clearly.

31. To seem limitless.

32. Something felt deeply and sincerely

33. A place where you cannot go.

34. To solve a mystery.

35. To ask to be left alone and not be bothered about something.

36. To earn exactly what was spent.

a. out of bounds
b. kick the bucket
c. the benefit of the doubt
d. by the book
e. catch your breath
f. give me a break
g. know no bounds
h. rock the boat
i. get to the bottom of
j. from the bottom of your heart
k. break even
l. a breath of fresh air
m. beat around the bush
n. go broke
o. funny business

25.	
26.	
27.	
28.	
29.	
30.	
31.	
32.	
33.	
34.	
35.	
36.	

D. Fill in the gaps with the correct Idiom.

1.

A: "Okay, I've been listening to you for almost twenty five minutes, but I'm still not at all sure what you're asking me! Don't **(37)** .... , say what you mean! I'm waiting for you to hit the ball into my court, so to speak, but it seems to me that you've hit the ball **(38)**......................... instead! I don't know how to respond! You're obviously worried about something and we need to **(39)**........................... . I hope there's no **(40)**......................... going on and that you're not trying to say now that you can't supply the jewellery we commissioned you to make for our shop."

B: "No, nothing like that! I'm sorry I'm being unclear. It's just that I need your help, and I feel a bit uncomfortable asking. You see, I underestimated the costs for the last job I did, and I only just **(41)**.................. . I didn't make a profit at all. Now, if I buy the materials to make the jewellery you've ordered I will **(42)**............. . I won't have any money for food! So, you see, I'm rather stuck. I wanted to ask if you could give me half of my pay as an advance so that I can buy materials. Is this possible?"

A: "Well, yes. That's no problem at all. Your designs have been **(43)**................................ for our shop, and if we can make it easier for you to get more to us, we'll be happy to!"

B: "What a relief! Your understanding **(44)**............................ and I am grateful **(45)**................................. !"

A: "It's nothing, really! We've been very happy with your work in the past."

2.

A: "Oh my! It made me **(46)**............................ when I saw you sitting there like that, so still! I thought for a minute that you had **(47)**............................ ."

B: "**(48)**............................ ! Surely I'm not looking so old and unwell! I was just having a nap!"

27

Illustrated Idioms

E. Do the CrossWord Puzzle, finding the correct IDIOM from Unit 4.

ACROSS

49. I don't want to find out that there was any funny .... going on!
50. The area of the school yard surrounded by a green fence is out of .... to children under 10.
51. If I sell this house for any less, I won't manage to break ....
52. She has trouble speaking her mind and always seems to beat around the ....
53. The new student was like a breath of .... in the classroom.
54. If you don't start taking care of yourself you're going to kick the .... before you're forty!

DOWN

55. I'm not sure, but I will get to the .... soon.
56. If you don't give me a .... and stop lecturing me about what I eat, I will stop visiting you.
57. His knowledge seems to know no ....
58. If you keep borrowing money using a credit card, you can easily go ....
59. No, it's true! I mean it from the bottom of my ....
60. People always catch their .... when they first see this view.

UNIT 5

IDIOMS

have butterflies	mind your own business	go like hot cakes
have your cake and eat it	lay your cards on the table	have all the cards
play cat and mouse with someone	catch someone red-handed	when the cat's away the mice will play
like chalk and cheese	let the cat out of the bag	what's the catch

have butterflies - You have butterflies if you have a nervous feeling in your stomach. e.g. *I always have butterflies before speaking in public.*

mind your own business - You mind your own business when you concentrate on matters which concern you, and don't pay attention to, or interfere in, other people's affairs.
e.g. *"How did you vote in the last election?" "Mind your own business."*

go like hot cakes - Something that is going like hot cakes is so popular that it is selling quickly because a lot of people are buying it. e.g. *Cards depicting Santa are going like hot cakes this December.*

have your cake and eat it - If someone wants to have their cake and eat it, they want to do or have two things not usually possible together, instead of choosing one and being content.
e.g. *You can't take a high responsibility job and then go on holiday at short notice; the world doesn't work that way! You can't have your cake and eat it!*

lay your cards on the table - You lay your cards on the table when you make your intentions known, rather than trying to keep them secret.
e.g. *I think you need to lay your cards on the table and tell me exactly what you're expecting of me.*

have all the cards - If you have all the cards you have an advantage which puts you in control of a situation. e.g. *I think my landlord has all the cards. I'm not going to move, whether he fixes the door or not, and he knows it.*

like chalk and cheese - Two things or people that are like chalk and cheese are completely different.
e.g. *The twins are like chalk and cheese; one very quiet and observant, and the other loud and active!*

play cat and mouse with someone - If someone plays cat and mouse with a person less powerful than themselves, they tease them by repeatedly making them afraid and then letting them relax. e.g. *I think one of them is playing cat and mouse with the other; they keep talking about getting married, then breaking up, over and over again!*

let the cat out of the bag - You let the cat out of the bag if you accidentally give away information which is supposed to remain a secret.
e.g. *Be careful not to let the cat out of the bag; I want this party we're planning to be a surprise.*

catch someone red-handed - You catch someone red-handed when you find them in the act of doing something forbidden.
e.g. *Tommy was taking candy without permission, and his mother caught him red-handed.*

when the cat's away the mice will play - If someone says "when the cat's away, the mice will play", they mean that when the person who is normally in authority is absent, people will take advantage of the situation. e.g. *When the cat's away the mice will play; since the boss is off sick, let's go to the pub for the afternoon!*

what's the catch / what the catch is - People ask "what's the catch?" if they think there must be a problem with something that seems too good, or is too easy to obtain.
e.g. *When Michael does the dishes without being asked I always wonder what the catch is.*

Illustrated Idioms

A. Fill in the gaps in the sentences below with the correct Idiom from Unit 5.

1. I wish he would .... and stop trying to read over my shoulder!

2. You can't .... too; you've got no chance of being both a football star AND an astronaut.

3. Timothy is sure to win because he ....

4. She .... before she sat the exam.

5. These new strawberry popsicles are popular; in fact, they're ....

6. I'd be greatful if you'd just .... , and stop trying to confuse me!

Unit 5

7. Mum and Dad found out she was smoking when her little sister ....

8. I know that .... so I'm sure my kids are going to throw a party as soon as I leave!

9. "I'll give it to you completely free of charge."
"Really? So .... ?"

10. The Government is .... with political prisoners, releasing and then re-imprisoning them.

11. The robber was .... when the policeman spotted him climbing out of the window.

12. Mr. and Mrs Jones were a funny sight when they went out together because they were ....

Illustrated Idioms

B. Choose the correct answer A, B, C or D.

13. They know I .... in this situation, so I doubt that they will make any demands.
    a. have butterflies
    b. have all the cards
    c. let the cat out of the bag
    d. mind my own business

14. Since the night patrols started in rural areas, several cattle thieves have ....
    a. gone like hot cakes
    b. laid their cards on the table
    c. had their cake and eaten it
    d. been caught red-handed

15. The two cities .... ; I can't believe they are only 50 miles apart and so different!
    a. have all the cards
    b. are like chalk and cheese
    c. are going like hot cakes
    d. are playing cat and mouse with me

16. I didn't know their engagement was a secret and I'm afraid I ....
    a. laid my cards on the table
    b. let the cat out of the bag
    c. played cat and mouse with them
    d. minded my own business

17. No thanks, I don't want a coffee before my performance; I already .... and that will just make it worse!
    a. have all the cards
    b. laid my cards on the table
    c. have butterflies
    d. have my cake and eat it

18. If she tells me I'm raising my children the wrong way one more time, I will tell her ....
    a. to mind her own business
    b. when the cat's away the mice will play
    c. to play cat and mouse with me
    d. to have her cake and eat it

19. This flight is half the price of the others, but I wonder: '..................' ?
    a. who let the cat out of the bag
    b. when the cat's away will the mice play
    c. what's the catch
    d. do I have all the cards

20. You can't expect your children to behave if you leave them unsupervised; ....
    a. you will be caught red-handed
    b. mind your own business
    c. lay your cards on the table
    d. when the cat's away the mice will play

21. You'd better buy that jacket if you want it; .... ! They will probably sell out soon.
    a. you have all the cards
    b. it's like chalk and cheese
    c. they're going like hot cakes
    d. what's the catch

22. I'm going to .... We've offered the job to someone else, but if he doesn't accept it by Friday, we will offer it to you.
    a. lay my cards on the table
    b. have my cake and eat it
    c. play cat and mouse with you
    d. mind my own business

23. Don't .... ! Either come with me to Paris or not, but don't keep saying maybe yes, and then maybe no!
    a. be like chalk and cheese
    b. catch me red-handed
    c. play cat and mouse with me
    d. let the cat out of the bag

24. Some painters actually do make money, so you may be able to ....
    a. lay your cards on the table
    b. let the cat out of the bag
    c. have all the cards
    d. have your cake and eat it

Unit 5

C. Match the Definitions with the correct Idiom. There are 3 extra Idioms that do not match with any Definition.

25. To have a nervous feeling in your stomach.

26. To concentrate on your own affairs and not those of others.

27. To sell quickly.

28. To want two things that it is not possible to have at the same time.

29. To make your intentions known rather than keep them secret.

30. To have an advantage which puts you in control of a situation.

31. To tease by making someone afraid then letting them relax.

32. To accidentally give away secret information.

33. To find someone doing something forbidden.

34. When someone in authority is absent, people will take advantage of their absence.

35. When two things or people are completely different.

36. To ask why something seems too good or too easy.

25.	
26.	
27.	
28.	
29.	
30.	
31.	
32.	
33.	
34.	
35.	
36.	

a. out of bounds
b. have all the cards
c. go like hot cakes
d. mind your own business
e. lay your cards on the table
f. catch someone red-handed
g. what's the catch?
h. a bird in the hand
i. get to the bottom of
j. play cat and mouse with someone
k. like chalk and cheese
l. have butterflies
m. let the cat out of the bag
n. have your cake and eat it
o. when the cat's away the mice will play

D. Fill in the gaps with the correct Idiom.

1.
My brother and I are (37).................................. . No one ever believes that we're related. I was an obedient child and he was always getting (38).................................. doing something he wasn't supposed to. He loves to be the centre of attention and wants to be an actor one day. Dad always likes to remind him that he can't (39).................................. , so if he wants to be a successful actor he will have to work very hard and stop sleeping late in the mornings! I, on the other hand, (40).................................. if I have to stand up and give a presentation to my colleagues. Acting, for me, would be a nightmare! I can keep a secret though, but if you tell my brother anything, he will inevitably (41).................................. and everyone will know about it in a week. I prefer to (42).................................. and I'm sure I would never gossip about other people.

2.
A: "Good morning Mr. Jamison. Do you know why I've called you into my office?"

B: "No, Mr. Baker, I don't. Last week you gave me a warning for being late with the design for the new clothing line advertisement, then after I finished and we published it, you praised me and said the new line was (43).................................. because of my work. Now, from the tone of your e-mail, I think you are unhappy. I hope you will just (44).................................. now, and not continue to (45).................................. ."

A: "Well, Mr. Jamison, I have a very serious matter to bring up with you, but don't worry, I think you will find it to be good news. We've decided to promote you to head designer for department four."

B: "Really? This is a supprise! So, (46).................................. ?"

A: "There isn't one, you see, you (47).................................. in this matter. We are depending on you. However, you will have to manage others and this is not easy. It will be a new responsibility for you. Remember that at any supervising position (48).................................. ! So, you need to manage your staff carefully."

33

Illustrated Idioms

E. Do the CrossWord Puzzle, finding the correct IDIOM from Unit 5.

ACROSS

49. I'm sure you will get your way because you have all the ....
50. I'm so nervous about meeting the Prime Minister that I have ....
51. I can't believe it! What's the ....
52. One day we will catch you .... and then you'll get what you deserve.
53. Watch what you say so that you don't let the cat .... !

DOWN

54. You're too nosey. Why don't you mind your own .... ?
55. Don't play .... with your little brother; you'll upset him!
56. They are very unlikely friends; like chalk and ...., personality wise!
57. You are not being realistic. You can't have your cake and ....
58. If you'd just lay your cards on the .... , I might be able to help you.
59. They are the newest thing and they're going like ....
60. I don't like to leave my children with a sitter because when the cat's away the.................... .

34

Review
Units 1-5

Illustrated Idioms

A. Match the first half of the sentence with the second half containing the correct Idiom.

1. I was getting tired of listening to Katy complain when the phone rang and I was
2. I thought skiing was easy, but perhaps it was just
3. Many tactics used in political campaigns are rather
4. I have no time for myself because I'm always
5. He's living there rent-free so he shouldn't complain;
6. Don't make me guess what you're thinking;
7. Okay, I'll wash the dishes if you will just
8. If you want to break up, please tell me! Don't
9. This sounds too good to be true;
10. He's very talented and his abilities seem to
11. You can't blame the kids for having a party; after all
12. I won't feel comfortable until we've
13. Your presence has really improved the mood here; it's
14. If you don't stop smoking and get some exercise you'll
15. Don't quit your job till you've found another;
16. Since her accident, she doesn't like to drive; you could say:
17. If you start running in the morning you'll lose weight and be more alert; this way you will
18. I don't know why I'm feeling so sad; I guess that I've just
19. I can't find my car keys! They seem to have
20. Now I see what you are doing! Sending e-mails, not working! I've

1.	
2.	
3.	
4.	
5.	
6.	
7.	
8.	
9.	
10.	
11.	
12.	
13.	
14.	
15.	
16.	
17.	
18.	
19.	
20.	

a. below the belt.
b. at his beck and call.
c. got the blues.
d. when the cat's away the mice will play.
e. beggars can't be choosers!
f. what's the catch?
g. saved by the bell.
h. a bird in the hand, remember!
i. got to the bottom of this mystery.
j. kill two birds with one stone.
k. beginner's luck.
l. kick the bucket!
m. vanished into thin air.
n. a breath of fresh air!
o. lay your cards on the table.
p. caught you in the act this time!
q. know no bounds.
r. once bitten, twice shy.
s. get off my back!
t. play cat and mouse with me!

Revision Test 1: Units 1-5

B. Write **C** or **I** (**Correct** or **Incorrect**) in the box to the left for each sentence using an Idiom.

21. When you arrive, be sure to ring a bell.
22. Jessica is in an awful mood; she must have got out of bed on the wrong side.
23. I hope you're over the flu and alive and kicking again right away!
24. If you're not sure how to make meat loaf, you'd better cook the books and find out.
25. My dog has turned me into an early bird; he wakes me to let him out every morning at 5am and I watch the sun rise.
26. Ever since I moved, there are some bits and pieces that I just can't find.
27. That new comedy really is funny business!
28. His wisdom is so great that it seems to be out of bounds.
29. Don't beat around the bush; if you're unhappy just say so!
30. The marathon has just begun and Tim is running so fast I'm afraid he will go broke.
31. The waterfall was so beautiful that I caught my breath.
32. Can't you just give me a break? I'm doing the best I can.
33. Really, I mean it from the bottom of my heart.
34. He tried to use my idea without giving me credit, but I caught him red-handed.
35. If we're lucky, it might have broken even and we can glue it back together.
36. It's a surprise, so be careful not to let the cat out of the bag!
37. Look at the runners! They are going like hot cakes around the field!
38. Don't give in; you have all the cards so they are sure to compromise.
39. You need to mind your own business; how much he earns is not your concern!
40. You were wrong and you should apologize because it's better safe than sorry.

Revision Test 1: Units 1-5

C. Fill in the gaps in the text with the correct form of the Idioms from the box below.

to no avail	on the ball	cost an arm and a leg	have butterflies
act your age	better late than never	no bed of roses	a blessing in disguise
stab someone in the back	have your cake and eat it	rock the boat	an ace up your sleeve
the ball's in your court	in the blink of an eye	for better or worse	get your act together
a bee in your bonnet	by the book	like chalk and cheese	give someone the benefit of the doubt

Jenny's mother didn't go to college; girls just didn't do that when she was growing up. Maybe that's why her mother always had (41).............................. about Jenny getting a good education. She did very little (42)..................... when it came to raising her daughter, and instead of taking dance classes like the other girls, Jenny took astronomy and chemistry classes at the museum. Jenny asked to take dance classes once, like the other girls did, but (43)................... . Her parents said "well you can if you want, but then you'll have to stop your astronomy classes; unfortunately you can't (44)............................... because we can't afford to send you to both! Classes are expensive, they (45).............................. ! But the (46).............................. ; it's entirely your choice!" And so, (47)............................. , Jenny gave up the idea of dance classes quickly, (48)............................... actually, because she really liked astronomy.

I think sometimes Jenny would have preferred to (49).................... and watch cartoons, for example, instead of reading classic literature on a Sunday morning, and sometimes she seemed so different from her peers that you could say they were (50)................................. . However, she was an agreeable child and didn't (51)...................... much. But she wasn't timid, so if she was actually unhappy, (52)..................................... , I'd say she probably would have said something.

You could say that her unusual upbringing was (53).................................. because when she got older she was always (54).................. in school, and did very well academically. All the knowledge she had acquired as a child gave her (55)............................. . However, her time in school was (56)........................ because some students were jealous of her good grades and constantly tried to (57)............................... .

Of course, she went to university. And when she was there, she signed up for dance classes. At first she found them difficult and, in fact, she was so nervous that she (58)........................ for the first few classes. But she was determined to (59)................................ and learn how to dance; after all, (60).............................. !

UNIT 6

IDIOMS

cash in your chips	hard cheese	out cold
in a class of your own	against the clock	under a cloud
every cloud has a silver lining	come in from the cold	off colour
add colour to something	two's company, three's a crowd	(pass) with flying colours

cash in your chips - To die.
e.g. I think you'd better make your will; after all, you never know when you might cash in your chips!

hard cheese - If someone says "hard cheese", it is a rude way of saying that you will just have to accept a situation, whether you like it or not. It's like saying 'tough luck' or 'bad luck'.
e.g. You're bored? Hard cheese! You have to go to the gym; you can't lose weight by sitting on the sofa!

every cloud has a silver lining - If you say that every cloud has a silver lining, you mean that there is always a positive side to every situation, however bad it may seem.
e.g. Now you've lost your job, at least you'll have more time for the kids. Every cloud has a silver lining.

in a class of your own - If you consider that someone or something is in a class of their (or its) own, you think that they (or it) are (is) much better than any other person / thing in a particular area of activity or for a particular purpose.
e.g. Shakespeare was in a class of his own; none of the other playwrights' works from that period have stood the test of time so well.

against the clock - When you do something against the clock, you are doing it as fast as you can and recording how long it takes you, or you are working under pressure to meet a specific deadline.
e.g. I don't care how fast Theresa swam; I'm competing against the clock, not against my team mates!

under a cloud - If you are under a cloud, you are in trouble for something which you have done previously and which has caused strong disapproval.
e.g. I don't know the exact circumstances of her resignation, but she left under a bit of a cloud.

out cold - Unconscious.
e.g. You must have been really tired because as soon as you sat down you were asleep; it was like you were out cold!

come in from the cold - When someone comes in from the cold, they re-enter a group or rejoin an activity after a period of time when they were not permitted to do so, or they are welcomed back into a group after a period of self-imposed isolation.
e.g. Allegations of misconduct were dropped and the MP came back in from the cold.

off colour - If you are off colour, you are not feeling very well, but you are not seriously ill either.
e.g. Are you sure you're feeling alright? You look rather off colour.

add colour to something - Something that adds colour to something else brings some energy, interest or variety to that thing.
e.g. All the different ethnicities of the people here add a lot of colour to the neighbourhood.

two's company, three's a crowd - If someone says "two's company, three's a crowd", they mean that, in their opinion, two people are more likely to be happy together than a group of three.
e.g. My brother wants to go everywhere with us but he's old enough to understand that sometimes two's company and three's a crowd!

(to pass) with flying colours - To complete something (a task or test) with flying colours is to do it very easily and very successfully. This idiom is usually accompanied by the verb "to pass".
e.g. Mary passed her entrance exams with flying colours.

Illustrated Idioms

A. Fill in the gaps in the sentences below with the correct Idiom from Unit 6.

1. "I don't want to come to the shops with you."
"................., you're coming."

4. The old man .... last week. The funeral's on Friday.

2. Natalie was .... We'll never see a dancer like her again at this institution.

5. If he'd stayed in university, he wouldn't have started his business at such a lucky time; see, ... !

3. James was .... for a few weeks after he missed a critical goal and caused the team to lose.

6. Laura is doing an arduous ten kilometre run preceded by a long assault course, all ....

Unit 6

7. Tom felt that he had .... when his broken leg healed and he could play on the team again.

10. I saw him fall, but by the time I got to him he was ....

8. His enthusiastic lecturing style .... to a subject that many people regard as dull.

11. I've been feeling a bit .... ever since I came back from my holiday.

9. She passed her exams ....

12. No, sorry, I'd rather you didn't come with us. ....

Illustrated Idioms

B. Choose the correct answer A, B, C or D.

13. She's .... and we can't revive her; we'd better call an ambulance!
    a. under a cloud
    b. hard cheese
    c. out cold
    d. off colour

14. You should try .... your speech to keep the audience's attention.
    a. against the clock
    b. to cash in your chips in
    c. to add colour to
    d. with flying colours

15. "You don't look too well - do you feel OK?" "No, I feel rather .... today."
    a. in a class of my own
    b. under a cloud
    c. off colour
    d. out cold

16. We are always working .... in order to get the newspaper to the printer on time.
    a. under a cloud
    b. in a class of our own
    c. with flying colours
    d. against the clock

17. After being estranged from the family for several years, Bill finally .... and returned one Christmas.
    a. came in from the cold
    b. cashed in his chips
    c. was out cold
    d. went against the clock

18. I feel as if I've been .... in the shop all week ever since the manager found out that I overcharged a customer.
    a. against the clock
    b. under a cloud
    c. off colour
    d. in a class of my own

19. Try not to worry, because .... and it may still turn out for the best.
    a. you'll come in from the cold
    b. you're hard cheese
    c. two's company and three's a crowd
    d. every cloud has a silver lining

20. He is becoming a very good actor; he was equal to the test of that very challenging role, which he passed ....
    a. under a cloud
    b. with flying colours
    c. in a class of his own
    d. against the clock

21. As a mathematician, Jane is .... ; she's the only one consistently thinking outside the box.
    a. in a class of her own
    b. with flying colours
    c. coming in from the cold
    d. off colour

22. How can I make her understand that .... without hurting her feelings?
    a. every cloud has a silver lining
    b. she's in a class of her own
    c. she's coming in from the cold
    d. two's company, three's a crowd

23. If you're trying to tell me you don't have time, well, ... ! Every one of us is busy!
    a. cash in your chips
    b. hard cheese
    c. come in from the cold
    d. two's company, three's a crowd

24. A: "You've been going home a lot lately."
    B: "Yes, I want to spend time with my grandfather. He's 90 now, and you never know when he might ...."
    a. cash in his chips
    b. come in from the cold
    c. go against the clock
    d. be in a class of his own

Unit 6

C. Match the Definitions with the correct Idiom. There are 3 extra Idioms that do not match with any Definition.

25. To die.

26. To rudely tell someone to just accept the situation.

27. There is a good side to every situation.

28. Much better at something than all the others.

29. To do something as fast as possible and record the time it takes.

30. In trouble for something you have done that caused strong disapproval.

31. Unconscious.

32. To join in an activity or group again after not being able/permitted to for some time.

33. Not very well, but not very ill either.

34. To bring energy, interest or variety to something.

35. To imply that two people will have a better time than three people will.

36. To overcome a challenge easily and with total success.

25.	
26.	
27.	
28.	
29.	
30.	
31.	
32.	
33.	
34.	
35.	
36.	

a. off colour
b. add colour to something
c. hard cheese
d. beggars can't be choosers
e. the ball's in your court
f. come in from the cold
g. pass with flying colours
h. two's company, three's a crowd
i. alive and kicking
j. every cloud has a silver lining
k. cash in your chips
l. in a class of your own
m. out cold
n. under a cloud
o. do it against the clock

D. Fill in the gaps with the correct Idiom.

1.
It's been a rather eventful day. I was training for the marathon next week, and I was pushing myself fairly hard because I was running **(37)**........................... , trying to improve my time. However I'd been feeling a little **(38)**................ since I woke up, and then suddenly I was **(39)**............... ! My friend, who I was running with, said I just fell over without any warning at all! He said it was so sudden and dramatic that he was worried I'd actually **(40)**................................., so he called for an ambulance but I was fine again by the time it had arrived; just a little embarrassed. I went to the hospital anyway and got checked out, but they couldn't find anything wrong, and just told me to eat plenty of carbohydrates and drink water.

I'm not feeling very confident now, but my friend tells me not to worry, that I'm **(41)**................................... and even if I don't manage my best time I will probably still win easily and overcome the challenge **(42)**............................... . I think he is exaggerating a bit, but I will just go and do my best.

And by chance, while I was at the hospital, they checked my vision and told me that I need glasses! I guess I should be able to see much better than I do, and I didn't even realise until now! My new glasses might even stop me from getting headaches. That would be nice. I guess **(43)**... .

2.
A: "My sister and her new husband are going to the Canary Islands in June. I would love to go along - I've hardly seen them since they got married - so I keep asking them to let me **(44)**........................ and join them! The first time I brought it up, they told me "**(45)**.. ." When I tried to explain to them that they were wrong, and I would **(46)**..................... to their holiday because I'm always meeting people and making new friends, and they would surely get bored spending two weeks just with each other, they told me "**(47)**........................... ! You are NOT coming!" When I asked them again yesterday they completely ignored me! They didn't even speak to me. So very rude! I feel like I'm **(48)**........................... with them now. I just don't understand it!"

B: "Well, somehow it doesn't surprise me at all. I think you'd better let them alone!"

Illustrated Idioms

E. Do the CrossWord Puzzle, finding the correct IDIOM from Unit 6.

ACROSS

49. It was nice that you finally decided to come in .... ! We've missed you at our meetings.
50. Alison adds .... any party she goes to.
51. Something good will come of this; every cloud has a ....
52. "I want to go home." "Hard .... ! We are all staying until it's finished."
53. You will pass with flying .... ; I know it!
54. Do you know what to do for someone who is out .... ?
55. What an amazing performance! You're really in a class of ....

DOWN

56. They'll forgive you eventually; you won't be under a .... forever.
57. I asked if I could join them at the table, but apparently two is company, ...
58. I suggest you should try working against the .... to see how much you can earn per hour.
59. I'm not feeling my best; a bit off .... , actually .
60. Have you heard? Our poor old neighbour Dora cashed in her .... last night.

44

UNIT 7

IDIOMS

hold in contempt	all things considered	too many cooks spoil the broth
tough cookie	keep your cool	cool as a cucumber
under the counter	just (a)round the corner	count me in
couch potato	crocodile tears	give someone the creeps

hold in contempt - If you hold someone or something in contempt, you have no respect at all for them / it.
e.g. *He holds all violence in the utmost contempt.*

all things considered - You say that something is the case, all things considered, when you are giving a general opinion after thinking about the whole situation.
e.g. *All things considered, I think you could do worse than rent this house.*

too many cooks spoil the broth - When so many people are trying to help with a job that they are all getting in each other's way, you can say "too many cooks spoil the broth".
e.g. *We both love gardening, but we don't work in the garden together; too many cooks spoil the broth. We take turns, instead.*

tough cookie - If you call someone, usually a woman, a tough cookie, you mean that she is hard, independent, and unlikely to worry about the feelings of others.
e.g. *She may not look like it, but she's one tough cookie; try to push her around at your own risk.*

keep your cool - Someone who keeps their cool remains calm in a difficult situation.
e.g. *He kept his cool and worked at the lock until he had finally broken through.*

cool as a cucumber - Someone who is as cool as a cucumber is very calm and collected in a given situation or as a general truth.
e.g. *Look at Miles! Everyone is running around in a panic and he sits there, cool as a cucumber!*

under the counter - Something that is sold under the counter is sold secretly and illegally.
e.g. *Since the government increased taxes, more people are buying alcohol under the counter.*

just (a)round the corner - An event which is just round (or around) the corner is going to happen very soon. e.g. *Spring is just round the corner.*

count me in - If you say to a person or a group of people "count me in", you mean that you want to be involved in something they are planning.
e.g. *You can count me in; I've looked over your business plan and it seems solid.*

couch potato - If you call someone a couch potato, you mean that they are very lazy and never do anything physically active.
e.g. *Get up and go outside to play! No child of mine is going to be a couch potato!*

crocodile tears - When someone pretends to cry or claims to feel sad because that is what people expect, or in order to obtain something for themselves, you say they are shedding crocodile tears.
e.g. *Those are crocodile tears for sure; Michelle never even met this uncle who has just died.*

give someone the creeps - If someone or something gives you the creeps, you have strong negative feelings about it (them), because it (they) seems (seem) strange and possibly dangerous or scary.
e.g. *This place really gives me the creeps. I can't stand the smell and the darkness in here.*

Illustrated Idioms

A. Fill in the gaps in the sentences below with the correct Idiom from Unit 7.

1. It rained the whole time but, ..., we had a good weekend.

2. She was gaining a reputation as a ...., a determined career girl who refused to be deflected from her dreams.

3. He arrived half an hour late and ....

4. Though they may have been too young to understand class, these rich kids already .... the poor ....

5. Thanks for offering, but we've got lots of volunteers, already. As they say, ...

6. I thought she'd be stressed working around the clock for so long, but she seems to be ....

Unit 7

7. Can you believe that 2009 is .... ?!

10. He used to slip me some cigarettes .... for wholesale prices.

8. After he lost his job, John became a ...., sitting in front of the television all day.

11. .... for the trip to London next week.

9. For some reason I feel like I'm being stared at and it's .... !

12. I think she sheds .... for the disadvantaged, but is basically happy with things the way they are.

Illustrated Idioms

B. Choose the correct answer A, B, C or D.

13. If you don't get a receipt, you could be accused of buying ....
    a. all things considered
    b. tough cookies
    c. crocodile tears
    d. under the counter

14. We both thought we knew best how to decorate the office, and look at it now; .... !
    a. cool as a cucumber
    b. just around the corner
    c. too many cooks spoil the broth
    d. all things considered

15. If those are .... , they are really convincing!
    a. couch potatoes
    b. crocodile tears
    c. tough cookies
    d. all things considered

16. His twenty first birthday is .... now!
    a. held in contempt
    b. under the counter
    c. just round the corner
    d. counted in

17. I must stop being .... and get more exercise because I feel awful.
    a. cool as a cucumber
    b. under the counter
    c. a couch potato
    d. held in contempt

18. I'm exhausted, but ...., it has been a successful day.
    a. keep your cool
    b. just round the corner
    c. count me in
    d. all things considered

19. I admire him because I think there is truly no one that ....
    a. counts him in
    b. he gives the creeps
    c. he keeps his cool
    d. he holds in contempt

20. She's .... ; if you yell at her, she'll probably cry!
    a. no tough cookie
    b. a couch potato
    c. cool as a cucumber
    d. crocodile tears

21. It's important to .... and not appear nervous at a job interview.
    a. count me in
    b. keep your cool
    c. hold me in contempt
    d. be a couch potato

22. If you're going to that great Indian restaurant you can .... !
    a. count me in
    b. give me the creeps
    c. keep your cool
    d. pay just round the corner

23. Although I'm sure she was angry, you couldn't tell; she remained ....
    a. a couch potato
    b. a tough cookie
    c. under the counter
    d. cool as a cucumber

24. "I don't have a good feeling about this place; ...."
    a. it's a tough cookie
    b. it gives me the creeps
    c. it keeps my cool
    d. it's under the counter

Unit 7

C. Match the Definitions with the correct Idiom. There are 3 extra Idioms that do not match with any Definition.

25. To have no respect for someone or something.

26. Thinking carefully about all aspects of a situation.

27. When so many people are helping with something that they get in each other's way.

28. A hard, independent woman.

29. To remain calm in a difficult situation.

30. Calm and collected.

31. Something sold secretly and illegally.

32. Happening soon or about to happen.

33. When you want to be involved in what I am planning.

34. Someone who never does any physical activity.

35. Crying or sadness that is not genuine.

36. To cause strong negative feelings.

25.	
26.	
27.	
28.	
29.	
30.	
31.	
32.	
33.	
34.	
35.	
36.	

a. keep your cool
b. tough cookie
c. hold in contempt
d. give someone the creeps
e. too many cooks spoil the broth
f. just around the corner
g. (a) couch potato
h. off colour
i. all things considered
j. under the counter
k. like chalk and cheese
l. count me in
m. cool as a cucumber
n. under a cloud
o. crocodile tears

D. Fill in the gaps with the correct Idiom.

1.
I'm not sure what to make of Julie. She is always perfectly polite, and (37)................................. ; I've never seen her lose her temper. She is one (38).................................. , that's for sure; she's ambitious, a good manager, and she knows how to get the results she wants. Yet, I sometimes feel like she (39).............. the rest of us .... because our positions in the company are below hers. It kind of (40).. when she's pleasant to us because I never know what she's really thinking. (41).. , I just don't trust her.

I had to go to her with a problem recently, because a girl I'm working with wouldn't do anything and I was having to do both our jobs and not succeeding, of course, and I was afraid I was going to get in trouble. She appeared quite sympathetic, but it was only (42)........................... I guess, because she did nothing. She basically told me to (43)................................. and just get on with it! I'm no (44)......................... , but I can't do the work of two full-time employees! It was a bit ruthless on her part. It didn't affect her directly, so she just didn't care.

2.
A: "Christmas is (45)..................................... now, so you need to make up your mind if you're coming with me to visit my family or not. I've found a ridiculously cheap flight, but I have to act quickly or it will sell out!"

B: "Are you sure the flight's not an (46)................................... deal? I don't trust some of these small package tour companies. Sometimes the flights they sell don't even exist!"

A: "No, I think you're being too extreme! I've travelled with this company before; they're legitimate. So, are you coming then?"

B: "I don't know. I don't really like big family events. Sometimes when everyone is making plans it's a case of (47).. and nobody has fun."

A: "We can do our own thing most of the time, don't worry."

B: "Okay, in that case you can (48)............................. . I'll come. "

Illustrated Idioms

E. Do the CrossWord Puzzle, finding the correct IDIOM from Unit 7.

ACROSS

49. She is successful because she is such a tough ....
50. Bill is always cool as a .... ; I've never seen him upset.
51. When I cook with my mum it's always a case of "too many cooks ...."
52. You can stop crying those crocodile .... now!
53. Racism is something we should all hold in ....
54. All things .... , I've had a fantastic year.

DOWN

55. That old house down the street gives me the ....
56. My cousin is a couch ....
57. Lisa can always keep her .... in an emergency.
58. My birthday is next week; just round the .... !
59. He offered to sell me cigarettes under the .... , but I refused.
60. I've made up my mind; I want to join you. You can .... !

UNIT 8

IDIOMS

have a crush on someone	have a cross to bear	not your cup of tea
a far cry from	curtains for someone	curiosity killed the cat
cut it out	cut someone dead	call it a day
look daggers	make someone's day	day in day out

have a crush on someone - Someone who has a crush on a certain person has fallen in love with that person in a rather childish and temporary way.
e.g. *He's talking about her all the time, but he only has a crush on her; I don't think this will lead to them getting married or anything.*

have a cross to bear - You have a cross to bear if you have a problem which you must accept, or deal with on your own.
e.g. *Although it seems ridiculous to her now, as a teenager she considered her big nose to be a terrible cross to bear.*

not your cup of tea - If something is not your cup of tea, it is not the type of thing which interests you.
e.g. *No, I'm afraid a fancy dress party is not really my cup of tea.*

a far cry from - Something which is a far cry from another thing is not at all similar to that thing.
e.g. *The public transportation here is a far cry from what we have at home; I don't know how people get by!*

curtains for someone - It is curtains for someone or something if the time of their/its end or death or downfall has come. e.g. *If that law passes, I'm afraid it's curtains for the European organisation.*

curiosity killed the cat - You tell someone that curiosity killed the cat to advise them not to ask any more questions.
e.g. *She wanted to know all about it, but I reminded her that curiosity killed the cat.*

cut it out - If you tell someone to "cut it out", you are telling them angrily to stop doing something.
e.g. *Would you cut it out? That tapping noise is really bothering me.*

cut someone dead - If someone cuts you dead, they pretend not to see you, or they refuse to greet you, as a way of showing dislike or anger towards you.
e.g. *Did you see that? He cut me dead; looked me in the eye and walked right by without saying anything!*

call it a day - You call it a day when you decide to stop working on something (usually temporarily to return to the task at a later time) or quit or give up a task / role / activity altogether.
e.g. *Let's call it a day. We can finish up what's left tomorrow morning.*

look daggers - You look daggers at someone if you look at them in a way that shows that you hate them, or that you are extremely angry with them.
e.g. *She didn't say a thing but I could tell she was furious because she was looking daggers at him!*

make someone's day - You make someone's day if you do something which makes them very happy.
e.g. *The news that they'd decided to come home at last really made my day.*

day in day out - Something that happens day in day out happens repeatedly and unchangingly.
e.g. *I can't believe I've been sitting here in the same office, day in day out, for nearly 20 years.*

Illustrated Idioms

A. Fill in the gaps in the sentences below with the correct Idiom from Unit 8.

1. Look, we're both facing challenges; you've got your ...., and I've got mine.

4. When she was fourteen, she .... huge .... her Technology teacher.

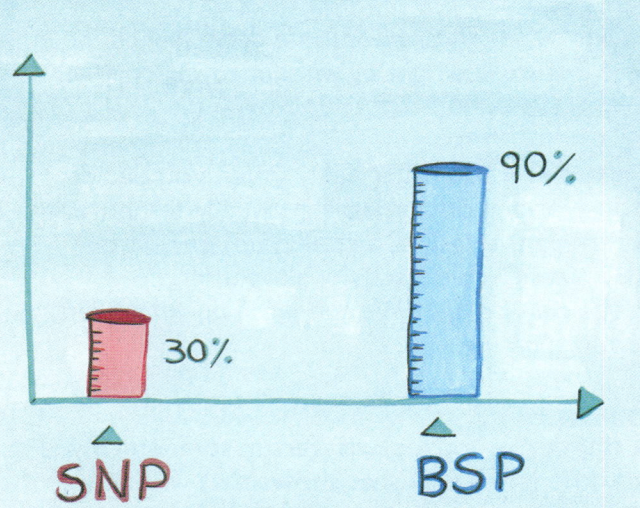

2. The BSP's lead over the SNP is now 60%; .... the close gap which separated them in January.

5. Joe said jazz was .... , but it looks like he's dancing and having a great time in spite of that!

3. It serves him right if he didn't like what he saw through the keyhole; after all .... !

6. It looks like it's .... Timothy; I don't think he'll be finishing the marathon now.

Unit 8

7. I knew it was him. "Stephen", I said. And he .... !

10. .... ! If you don't stop shouting and listen I'm going to hang up.

8. He was so angry after the accident that he was shouting and .... at me.

11. At 11pm we finally decided to .... and went home to get some sleep.

9. I could never live in that place; it rained .... the whole two weeks that I was there on holiday.

12. It .... when he dropped by and brought her flowers.

53

Illustrated Idioms

B. Choose the correct answer **A, B, C** or **D**.

13. Try to explain why you're angry; don't just sit there ....
    a. looking daggers at me
    b. day in day out
    c. cutting me dead
    d. making my day

14. If you don't mind, I'm going to .... because I have to be home by 6 o'clock.
    a. cut it out
    b. call it a day
    c. cut you dead
    d. make your day

15. This is .... the shop I was expecting from what I read on the advertisement.
    a. a far cry from
    b. curtains for
    c. day in day out
    d. curiosity killed the cat

16. This film may not be ...., but don't spoil it for everyone else by complaining!
    a. your cup of tea
    b. a cross to bear
    c. curtains for you
    d. a crush on you

17. Remember that .... and don't ask too many questions!
    a. you have a cross to bear
    b. you've made my day
    c. curiosity killed the cat
    d. he has called it a day

18. If they change our repertoire of music once more, that's it! It's .... ; I'm quitting the orchestra!
    a. going to make my day
    b. cutting me dead
    c. curiosity that killed the cat
    d. curtains for me

19. I wish you would .... ! I don't need to be reminded every 5 minutes to do the dishes!
    a. call it a day
    b. make my day
    c. cut it out
    d. have a cross to bear

20. Although it .... when he brings me coffee, I'll survive if he doesn't.
    a. is not my cup of tea
    b. looks daggers
    c. cuts him dead
    d. makes my day

21. Sorry, I didn't mean to .... ; it's just that I can't see more than a metre in front of me without my glasses.
    a. call it a day
    b. look daggers
    c. cut you dead
    d. make your day

22. When Stacy doesn't have a boyfriend she has a .... different every weekend!
    a. crush on someone
    b. cross to bear
    c. cup of tea
    d. day in day out

23. I'm sorry I can't help you. You see, I have my own .... and can't spare the money.
    a. cup of tea
    b. day in day out
    c. curtains for you
    d. cross to bear

24. Most people would become quite sad if they stayed at home .... and never went outdoors.
    a. making their day
    b. calling it a day
    c. day in day out
    d. curiosity killed the cat

Unit 8

C. Match the Definitions with the correct Idiom. There are 3 extra Idioms that do not match with any Definition.

25. To fall in love in a childish, temporary way.
26. To have a problem that you must accept.
27. Not the kind of thing that interests you.
28. Not at all similar to another thing.
29. Someone is about to end their time doing something, or die.
30. It is dangerous or unwise to ask too many questions.
31. To tell someone, angrily, to stop doing something.
32. To refuse to see or greet someone as a way of showing dislike.
33. To decide to put an end to a situation / activity.
34. To look at someone in a way that shows anger or hate.
35. To do something that makes someone very happy.
36. When something happens repeatedly without change.

a. not your cup of tea
b. against the clock
c. look daggers
d. make someone's day
e. (happening) day in day out
f. just around the corner
g. have a crush on someone
h. call it a day
i. a far cry from
j. cut it out
k. curiosity killed the cat
l. count me in
m. have a cross to bear
n. cut someone dead
o. curtains for someone

25.	
26.	
27.	
28.	
29.	
30.	
31.	
32.	
33.	
34.	
35.	
36.	

D. Fill in the gaps with the correct Idiom.

A: I'm afraid it might be **(37)**............................ their marriage. I saw them at a barbecue this weekend, and they were **(38)**............................ the happy couple I remember from years past. Nicole was **(39)**............................ at Bob all evening; it was impossible not to notice! And once when Bob tried to ask her something she **(40)**............................ and walked right out of the room. I don't know the details about what's wrong, of course, but Anna knows them really well and she says that staying at home just doesn't seem to be Bob's **(41)**............................ . He's always out at the pub and Nicole is tired of staying in by herself **(42)**............................ . I think he's drinking too much, and I heard that Nicole told him that if he didn't **(43)**............................ she was going to leave. Also, Anna said that he came home one night and accused Nicole of **(44)**............................ their neighbour! How ridiculous! Apparently that was when she decided to **(45)**............................ and not even try to work things out!"

B: "Well, if Bob is an alcoholic, it seems like he has quite a **(46)**............................ and probably needs help and support."

A: "True. I wonder if I should ask Nicole if she's tried to get him help for his drinking problem."

B: "No, I wouldn't do that. Somehow I don't think it would **(47)**............................ to know that we're all talking about her! And it's not really our business; **(48)**............................ after all! I'd leave it for her close friends and family to give her advice."

55

Illustrated Idioms

E. Do the CrossWord Puzzle, finding the correct IDIOM from Unit 8.

Across

49. Maria has a .... the drummer in that music band.
50. Tom has a cross .... because he is severely dyslexic.
51. It's getting late; let's call it ....
52. It was a far.................... the tropical islands in the tourist brochures.
53. "Can I ask you a personal question?" "OK, but remember curiosity .... !"

Down

54. It would make my .... if you could come.
55. It is usually .... any horse that breaks a leg.
56. Would you cut .... that noise? I'm trying to sleep!
57. In the desert it is hot, dry, and sunny, day in ....
58. I don't want to talk to him; I'm so angry that if I see him I'll probably cut him ....
59. Look! He's looking .... at Nancy! I wonder what she's done to him.
60. I'm afraid action movies are not my .... at all.

UNIT 9

IDIOMS

have seen better days	seize the day	cut a deal with someone
those were the days	a dog's life	make a big deal of something
a drop in the ocean	drop dead	bite the dust
allow the dust to settle	all ears	go in one ear and out the other

have seen better days - Something that has seen better days is not in very good condition.
e.g. *Well, the furniture's nice, but the carpet's seen better days.*

seize the day - If someone tells you to seize the day they are telling you to take every opportunity to learn and experience new things now, rather than wait until a later date.
e.g. *You should seize the day and travel while you are young.*

cut a deal with someone - You cut a deal with someone when you reach an agreement or make a bargain. e.g. *If you're considering buying them both, perhaps we can cut a deal and save you some money.*

those were the days - People say "those were the days!" when they are thinking about past times which seem pleasant in some way when compared to the present (which seems less pleasant).
e.g. *"I remember when a pint of Guinness cost 15p." "Mm, those were the days, eh?"*

a dog's life - Someone's life is described as a dog's life if they have to work very hard in order to survive, and have very few pleasures.
e.g. *It's a dog's life being a temporary worker, looking for a job every now and then, usually anything you can get, almost always in a different city.*

make a big deal of something - If someone makes a big deal of something, they exaggerate its seriousness or importance.
e.g. *I've been lucky, that's all. No need to make a big deal of it.*

a drop in the ocean - You describe something as a drop in the ocean if it seems a very small amount in relation to something else, or in relation to what is needed.
e.g. *We consumed an average of 8 pasta meals per head last year, a drop in the ocean compared to the Italians, who ate a massive 300 meals each.*

drop dead - You tell someone to "drop dead" if you are very angry with them, or if you think that what they have said is nonsense.
e.g. *"Drop dead, you silly old fool," said a woman.*

bite the dust - Someone or something bites the dust when they (it) finish(es) or give(s) up, no longer have (has) any use, or die(s).
e.g. *Another coal mine bit the dust today.*

allow the dust to settle - You allow the dust to settle when you let someone calm down before you try to do anything else about a situation, or when you allow some time to pass before deciding what to do about a situation next.
e.g. *If I were you I'd allow the dust to settle before going and asking them for my money back.*

go in one ear and out the other - When something goes in one ear and out the other, you don't listen to it carefully enough to remember it later.
e.g. *I told her what I thought she should do, but my advice went in one ear and out the other.*

all ears - You say you are all ears if you are listening very carefully.
e.g. *Okay, so tell me what's bothering you. I'm all ears.*

Illustrated Idioms

A. Fill in the gaps in the sentences below with the correct Idiom from Unit 9.

1. While Ms. Jones considered summer an opportunity to read a lot, Jim prefered to .... and go swimming.

4. It's my favourite dress, though I've had it for years and it's definitely ....

2. Remember all the picnics we had when we lived down south? .... !

5. I cut .... with the Mercedes salesman that knocked $5,000 off the price.

3. Her mother .... her winning the class debating contest.

6. It's .... working as a farm labourer; long days in the hot sun with very little rest.

Unit 9

7. Megan was so fed up that she told her boss to .... and then quit!

10. You may have put together one piece of the puzzle, but that's just .... ; there are plenty more.

8. You should .... , then apologise; I don't think it will do any good right now.

11. It looks like the coffee machine has .... !

9. He pretended not to be interested in the singing of the birds, but in reality, as the couple whispered together, he was .... !

12. His doctor told him to cut back on coffee, but it seems to have ....

Illustrated Idioms

B. Choose the correct answer **A**, **B**, **C** or **D**.

13. Though it may seem like .... , each individual choice you make can affect the environment.
    a. a dog's life
    b. a drop in the ocean
    c. those were the days
    d. they've seen better days

14. "I wish I was a student again."
    "Yeah, ..."
    a. those were the days
    b. I've seen better days
    c. seize the day
    d. it's a dog's life

15. Be careful; if you .... her now she will just expect a better price next time.
    a. make a big deal of
    b. allow the dust to settle on
    c. bite the dust from
    d. cut a deal with

16. Well, I think you should .... and use the money to go abroad for the summer; you can always buy a new car when you're older.
    a. seize the day
    b. cut a deal
    c. go in one ear
    d. drop dead

17. "Wow, that's an ugly dog!"
    "He's 15 years old now and he's .... but he's my loyal friend!"
    a. bit the dust
    b. all ears
    c. seen better days
    d. a dog's life

18. Let's take your car. Mine is about to ....
    a. drop dead
    b. allow the dust to settle
    c. see better days
    d. bite the dust

19. It's no use asking him to clean up. Everything I tell him .... !
    a. bites the dust
    b. has seen better days
    c. makes a big deal out of something
    d. goes in one ear and out the other

20. When I was ready to talk about what happened, thankfully he ....
    a. allowed the dust to settle
    b. was all ears
    c. cut a deal with me
    d. dropped dead

21. What an insane accusation! Why don't you just .... and leave me alone!
    a. bite the dust
    b. seize the day
    c. drop dead
    d. drop in the ocean

22. If you .... before bringing up the subject again, I'm sure the negotiations will have a better outcome.
    a. seize the day
    b. go in one ear and out the other
    c. allow the dust to settle
    d. make a big deal of them

23. I wish you wouldn't .... how pretty our daughter is; she's smart, too, after all!
    a. allow the dust to settle
    b. make a big deal of
    c. cut a deal with
    d. go in one ear and out the other

24. "If I have to type one more number into this database I'll lose it!"
    "It's .... , I know, but it's only 10am!"
    a. a drop in the ocean
    b. going in one ear and out the other
    c. a dog's life
    d. biting the dust

Unit 9

C. Match the Definitions with the correct Idiom. There are 3 extra Idioms that do not match with any Definition.

25. When something is not in very good condition.

26. To take every opportunity to learn and experience new things.

27. To reach a bargain or make an agreement.

28. What people say about past pleasant times.

29. A life full of work with few pleasures.

30. To exaggerate the seriousness or importance of something.

31. Something very small in relation to something else.

32. To rudely tell someone that what they say is nonsense, or that you're angry.

33. To die, quit, give up, or no longer be of any use.

34. To give someone time to calm down before trying to solve a situation.

35. When something is neither listened to carefully or remembered.

36. Listening very carefully.

25.	
26.	
27.	
28.	
29.	
30.	
31.	
32.	
33.	
34.	
35.	
36.	

a. bite the dust
b. drop dead
c. seize the day
d. a dog's life
e. allow the dust to settle
f. cut a deal with someone
g. those were the days
h. call it a day
i. all ears
j. look daggers
k. come in from the cold
l. it goes in one ear and out the other
m. a drop in the ocean
n. has seen better days
o. make a big deal of something

D. Fill in the gaps with the correct Idiom.

1.
My little sister told me to (37)........................ yesterday! Well, she's not so little anymore; she'll be 18 next week. I was rather shocked and hurt when it came out of her mouth, but now I think the whole conversation was quite funny! She earned a lot of money working last summer and she's trying to decide what to do with it. I guess I had a bit of a strong opinion about that! I told her she should (38)........................ and do something wild, like spend a year travelling around the world, and not just spend it all on clothes and makeup! At first she was fascinated by the idea and was (39)........................ but before long I could tell from her expression that the things I was saying were just (40)........................ ! I guess I came across as too bossy, because then she just burst out with it and told me to mind my own business, it was her money! I think I'll (41)........................ for a couple of weeks then bring it up again, in a less pushy way. I don't want her to make a mistake she'll regret.

2.
I'll admit it, I've (42)........................ ! But that's to be expected, after all, I'm getting on in years. And I've had (43)........................ ; you can see that in the lines on my face. Actually, I feel worse for the younger ones now, trying to make a living off of the land. It's more difficult these days with all the big farms, and rich owners. If you work on one of those you're just a slave really, an insignificant speck of dust, (44)........................ ! When I was a lad, the farms were all small and family owned, and you had a relationship with your employers, you became part of the family so to speak. They trusted you, and you trusted them. Ah, (45)........................ ! It's been years though since things were like that. The small family farms all (46)........................ back when the government (47)........................ the big companies, and they bought up all the land. Some owners don't even live in our country! My friend Jonathan works for a man he's never even met! He doesn't (48)........................ it; he says it doesn't change his life. He says he's ploughing a field whether his boss is in the mansion up the road, or 6 thousand miles away! But he's a young lad. He doesn't remember the old times.

61

Illustrated Idioms

E. Do the CrossWord Puzzle, finding the correct IDIOM from Unit 9.

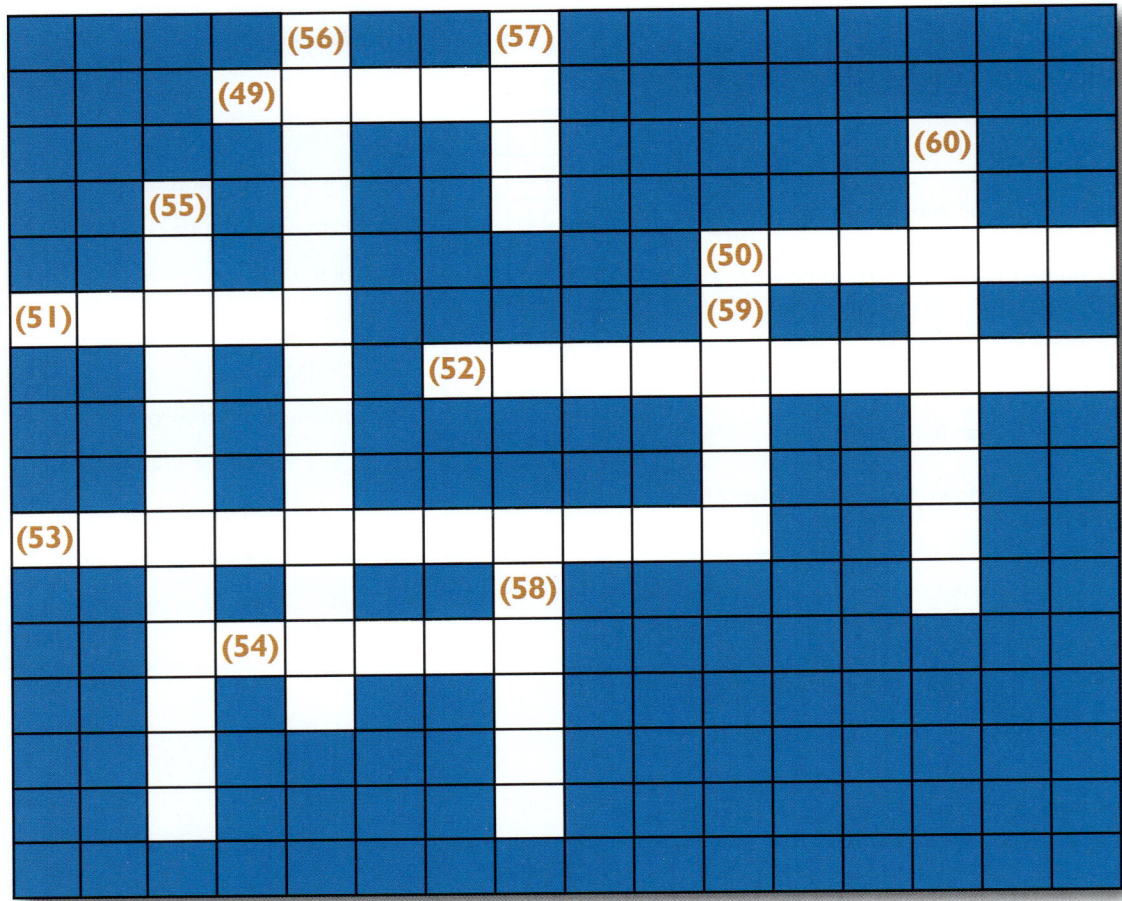

ACROSS

49. If you don't think I'm good enough, well, then you can just drop .... !
50. They think they're important, but on an international level they're just a drop in the ....
51. I'm afraid my old fridge is about to bite the ....
52. Don't make a .... his weight; it's not important.
53. Your coat looks like it's seen ....
54. It's a dog's .... in this city; all I ever do is work!

DOWN

55. I reminded her once but it went in one ear and ....
56. I think you'd better back off and allow the .... !
57. Seize the .... , because you might not get the chance again.
58. Okay, I'm all .... What did you want to tell me?
59. "I loved Christmas when I was a child!" "Yes, those were the .... !"
60. If you cut a .... them, they will probably do business with you again and again.

UNIT 10

IDIOMS

(have) an eye for something	keep an eye on	get even
a necessary evil	your own worst enemy	turn a blind eye
up to your ears	you can't teach an old dog new tricks	put all your eggs in one basket
(be) at a loose end	go easy on someone	take it easy

(to have) an eye for something - If someone has an eye for something he/she has a natural appreciation of that something, and the ability to apply that natural appreciation in a skilful way to his/her advantage.
e.g. *Mark is a painter who really has an eye for colour.*

keep an eye on - You are keeping an eye on people or things if you are watching them to make sure they are OK, or that they do not do anything wrong.
e.g. *Would you keep an eye on my bag while I pop into the toilet?*

get even - You get even, or get even with someone, when you do something to hurt or harm them as revenge for something they have done to hurt or harm you in the past.
e.g. *I had been waiting for years to get even with him, and then I saw my chance.*

a necessary evil - You say that something unpleasant is a necessary evil if you do not like it, but you have to accept it as a normal part of things.
e.g. *Negotiation is a necessary evil. It is the antithesis of open, honest communication.*

your own worst enemy - If someone creates severe problems for themselves by the way they behave, you sometimes say they are their own worst enemy.
e.g. *Her problems since then are all of her own making. You could say that she is her own worst enemy.*

turn a blind eye - You turn a blind eye, or turn a blind eye to something, if you decide to ignore it, or to pretend you cannot see it.
e.g. *I usually turn a blind eye to staff arriving a couple of minutes late.*

up to your ears - If you have so much of something to deal with that you cannot see how you are going to manage, you say that you are up to your ears in it. If you are up to your ears doing something specific, you are extremely busy doing that something specific.
e.g. *I've been up to my ears in work these past few weeks.*

you can't teach an old dog new tricks - If you say "you can't teach an old dog new tricks", you mean that it is very difficult to change old people's opinions, habits and behaviour.
e.g. *They say you can't teach an old dog new tricks, but I'm living proof that you can!*

put all your eggs in one basket - People sometimes tell you not to put all your eggs in one basket if they think that you are in danger of losing everything by depending on just one plan.
e.g. *Wisdom suggests that you shouldn't put all your eggs in one basket, so for most people a general distribution of investment is the wise choice.*

(to be) at a loose end - You are at a loose end if you have some spare time, but no idea what to do with it.
e.g. *So then, are we to suppose that being at a loose end leads to drunkenness and murder?*

go easy on someone - You go easy on someone when you do not punish or criticise them as severely as you could do, or when you show them more understanding than you normally would.
e.g. *I know he was wrong, but go easy on him. He's still very young.*

take it easy - You are taking it easy or taking things easy if you are relaxing or being careful not to work too hard.
e.g. *This year I'm determined to take it easy on weekends and not work every day.*

Illustrated Idioms

A. Fill in the gaps in the sentences below with the correct Idiom from Unit 10.

1. I'll .... the kids if you want to pop out to the shops.

4. Ernest has .... detail, so he arranged everything very carefully.

2. The new office buildings are horribly ugly, but they're .... I suppose.

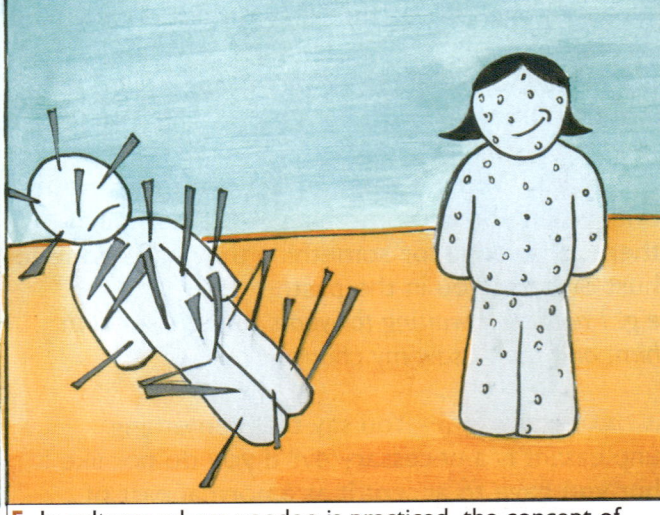

5. In cultures where voodoo is practiced, the concept of .... is of paramount importance.

3. Hugh .... to the no smoking sign in the cafe and lit up his cigarette anyway.

6. Maria is .... ; she is sure she will fail and she hasn't even begun yet!

Unit 10

7. We bought a new remote-controlled TV, but dad can't use the remote. I guess .... !

10. Between trying to get the ironing done and watching little Timmy play, Grandma was .... in work.

8. Brenden has been .... since he quit his job in June.

11. Don't.................................... , and I mean that literally! Here, let me help you carry the groceries.

9. The doctor told me to .... for a couple of weeks.

12. Don't let her talk to you like that! Here, give me the phone; I'll tell her to .... you for a change!

Illustrated Idioms

B. Choose the correct answer **A**, **B**, **C** or **D**.

13. If you suffer from stage fright, it helps to remember that you are usually ....
    a. at a loose end
    b. up to your ears
    c. a necessary evil
    d. your own worst enemy

14. I despise wearing a suit, but in my line of work it ....
    a. is taking it easy
    b. gets even
    c. is a necessary evil
    d. goes easy on me

15. Don't .... ; keep making other applications, too, because you might not get that job.
    a. turn a blind eye
    b. keep an eye on it
    c. put all your eggs in one basket
    d. teach an old dog new tricks

16. No matter how many times I explain how to send an e-mail to grandfather, he just doesn't get it. It's like trying to ....
    a. teach an old dog new tricks
    b. take it easy
    c. put all my eggs in one basket
    d. turn a blind eye

17. I hated working for that fashion agency; the whole time we were .... organising fashion shows!
    a. at loose ends in
    b. keeping an eye on
    c. up to our ears
    d. having an eye for

18. I hope you will .... Betty; she may be careless, but her intentions are always good.
    a. go easy on
    b. keep a blind eye on
    c. turn an eye to
    d. have an eye for

19. He's making things very difficult for me but I will .... in my own way by not letting it bother me at all!
    a. get even
    b. be up to my ears
    c. be my own worst enemy
    d. keep an eye on him

20. I'm .... right now so it would be no trouble at all to help you move.
    a. at a loose end
    b. taking it easy
    c. up to my ears
    d. my own worst enemy

21. You will not like travelling in India unless you can .... the poverty and squalor.
    a. go easy on
    b. keep an eye on
    c. turn a blind eye to
    d. get even with

22. Eliza .... style; she dresses impeccably and seems to surround herself with fashionable people.
    a. goes easy on
    b. turns a blind eye to
    c. keeps an eye on
    d. has an eye for

23. If you could .... you'd get more done because you can't work if you're exhausted.
    a. take it easy
    b. go easy on them
    c. be your own worst enemy
    d. put all your eggs in one basket

24. I'm ....my little brother so that my parents can go to the cinema tonight.
    a. getting even with
    b. up to my ears with
    c. going easy on
    d. keeping an eye on

Unit 10

C. Match the Definitions with the correct Idiom. There are 3 extra Idioms that do not match with any Definition.

25. To have natural appreciation of something which you can use to your advantage.

26. To watch a person or thing to make sure it is alright.

27. To hurt someone as revenge for something they have done to hurt you in the past.

28. Something you dislike but must accept as part of normal everyday life.

29. You are this when you have created your problems yourself.

30. To choose to ignore something.

31. Extremely busy.

32. A way to say it is difficult to change habits someone has had for a long time.

33. When you depend too much on one plan or option.

34. To have spare time but have no idea what to do with it.

35. To not punish or criticise someone as severely as you could.

36. To relax and not work too hard.

a. your own worst enemy
b. put all your eggs in one basket
c. be at a loose end
d. all ears
e. have an eye for
f. keep an eye on
g. cut a deal with someone
h. turn a blind eye
i. a necessary evil
j. a drop in the ocean
k. go easy on someone
l. take it easy
m. get even
n. up to your ears
o. you can't teach an old dog new tricks

25.	
26.	
27.	
28.	
29.	
30.	
31.	
32.	
33.	
34.	
35.	
36.	

D. Fill in the gaps with the correct Idiom.

You are definitely (37)... , Richard. You decided to (38)... and train to be a fine artist which is very specialised; if you're not successful enough to get shown in galleries, what will you do? It's not like a business major, where you can get a decent office job afterwards! Then, you act like you are (39).............................. and have nothing to do all day! You're (40).............................. when really, you should be (41).............................. in work. You have to finish 4 paintings this month, after all! Practice is a (42).............................. if you want to succeed at anything. Haven't you learned that yet? You're talented you know, you have an amazing (43)...................... composition. You need to make the most of that."

It's lucky for you that your professor (44).............................. and (45).............................. to your lazy ways! You'd be thrown out otherwise! But unfortunately that leaves me, your mother, to (46).............................. you! I'm getting too old for this now; I should just stop and let you find your own way. You're an adult now after all. I just can't see you making these mistakes and stay quiet though. I guess you (47).............................. . I'll (48).............................. though, I suppose, when I'm a bit older; then, it will be *your* turn to start worrying about me!

Illustrated Idioms

E. Do the CrossWord Puzzle, finding the correct IDIOM from Unit 10.

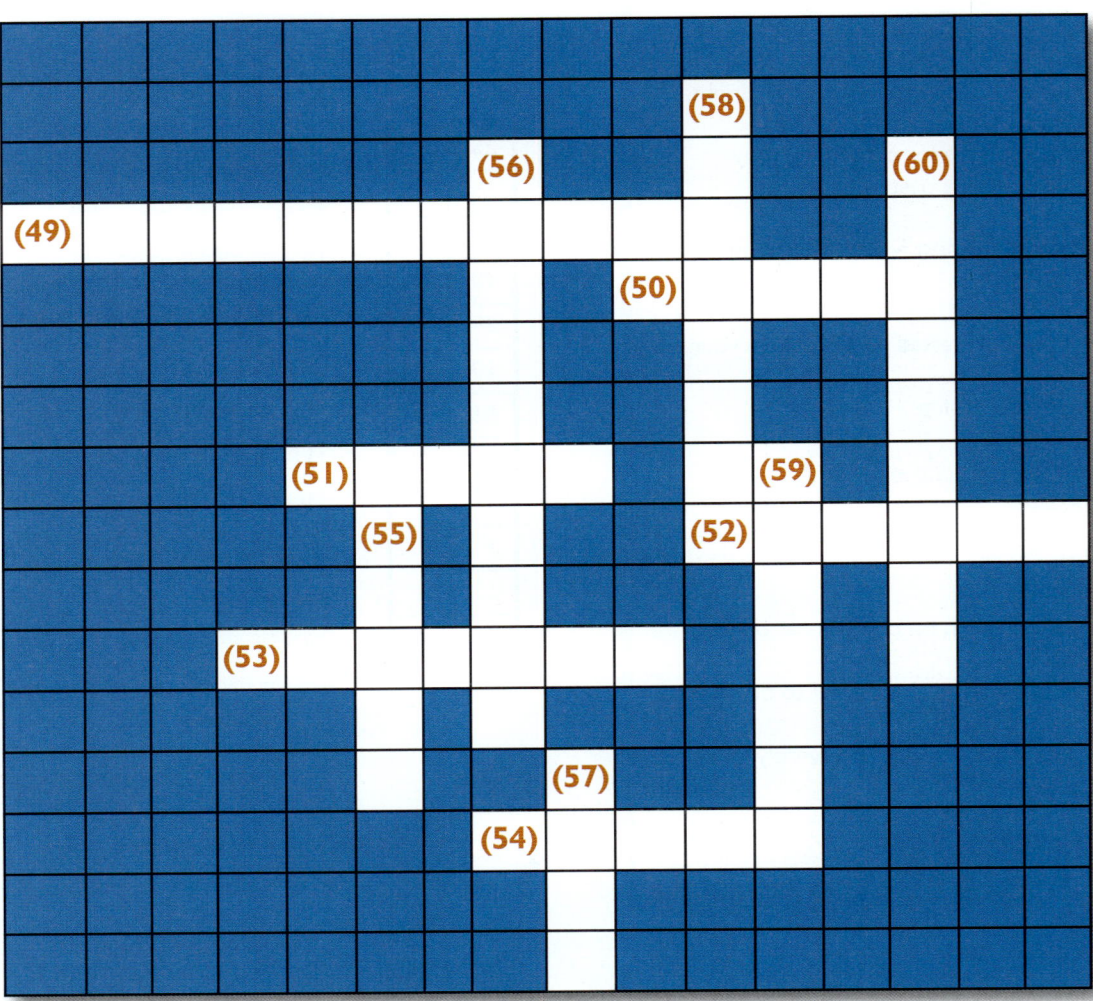

ACROSS

49. You're making things hard on yourself; actually you're your own ....
50. Those ugly mobile phone masts seem to be a necessary ....
51. No, don't bring anything; we're up to our .... in food already!
52. Keep an .... the weather if you go sailing; they're predicting gales.
53. It's risky to put all your eggs in one .... and invest only in stocks.
54. Her brother hit her, so she got .... by biting him.

DOWN

55. You look exhausted. You need to try to take it .... sometimes.
56. They say you can't teach an old dog ...., but my dad learns new computer skills more quickly than I do!
57. I'm at a loose .... this Saturday; do you want to go for a coffee?
58. Bob is bound to do well; he has a real .... good business opportunities.
59. Go .... Melanie; it's her first week here after all!
60. I usually turn a .... to the mess my neighbours make, but this is just too much.

Review

Units 6-10

Illustrated Idioms

A. Match the first half of the sentence with the second half containing the correct Idiom

1. There won't be another book in this series, I'm afraid; the author
2. He obviously hates me; I went to say hello and he
3. You should keep your options open; it's never wise to put
4. I have to work for another 3 hours even though I'm ready
5. I know you don't like maths;
6. The first step to having a healthier lifestyle is to stop
7. If you think this shirt matches I'll take your word because you have
8. You should take that indian cookery class; you will then
9. I worked in a factory for a year and one thing I'll say is it's
10. When I told him I was thinking about quitting my job in order to write full time, his only response was
11. Don't worry! This bad mark won't make much difference in the long term; it's
12. I think you're too strict; you should try to
13. Thanks for the offer but I have plenty of help;
14. If Jason gets a reputation for being difficult it could be
15. After working in many different cities, I
16. This trip you're planning sounds like a lot of fun. As long as it's not next weekend, you
17. I asked if she had put on weight and she's been
18. His doctor said he was suffering from exhaustion and he must
19. It seems a bit expensive but if they
20. "Do you remember your graduation?" "Yes, we had so much fun; ......"

a. came in from the cold and moved home.
b. to call it a day.
c. those were the days!
d. hard cheese! It's required.
e. seize the day!
f. curtains for his career, I'm afraid.
g. looking daggers at me ever since!
h. all your eggs in one basket.
i. cashed in his chips years ago.
j. too many cooks spoil the broth.
k. go easy on the children.
l. can count me in.
m. cut me dead!
n. cut a deal with me I'll buy it.
o. a dog's life, for sure.
p. add colour to our meals.
q. only a drop in the ocean.
r. being a couch potato.
s. take it easy for a while.
t. an eye for colour.

Revision Test 2: Units 6-10

B. Write **C** or **I** (**Correct** or **Incorrect**) in the box to the left for each sentence using an Idiom.

21. You're rich now, but be careful; evey cloud has a silver lining!
22. When I was confused and needed to talk to someone, Maryanne was all ears.
23. You need to get even and start living up to your responsibilities.
24. Uncle Tim has been under a cloud for years; the rest of the family hardly speaks to him.
25. I wouldn't take it too seriously; she's been known to shed crocodile tears before.
26. Drop dead! I've had enough of your nonsense!
27. We won't know for sure if we've successfully fixed the roof until we allow the dust to settle.
28. What awful weather! I've definitely seen better days!
29. It's not really your business; remember, curiosity killed the cat!
30. She's the best in her field; we all hold her in contempt.
31. If your grandfather doesn't want a credit card, don't force him. You can't teach an old dog new tricks.
32. We should bring our parents with us; after all two's company and three's a crowd.
33. Even if alcohol was banned, I'm sure it would still be available under the counter.
34. The bus was so crowded I'm afraid I had a crush on a stranger.
35. It's very important so you'd better cut it out and not lose it!
36. I occasionally do drink coffee, but it's not really my cup of tea.
37. Christmas is just around the corner and I haven't bought any presents yet.
38. He is an excellent student because everything goes in one ear and out the other.
39. I'll admit I made a mistake, but you don't have to make such a big deal of it.
40. She's her own worst enemy; sometimes, she's too independent.

Revision Test 2: Units 6-10

C. Fill in the gaps in the text with the correct form of the **Idioms** from the box below.

off colour	keep an eye on	up to our ears	bite the dust
cool as a cucumber	against the clock	a far cry from	kept my cool
at a loose end	turn a blind eye	out cold	with flying colours
gives me the creeps	all things considered	day in day out	cross to bear
made my day	in a class of their own	tough cookie	necessary evil

Usually, I would tell you that I love working as a school nurse, however some days, yesterday for example, it's (41).................... idyllic. As you know, school has just resumed after the summer holidays, so I'd been (42).................. for a while, but with this flu that's going around, we're (43).................... with patients now. Usually all I need to do is reassure the children, see that they have a quiet place to rest, and decide if their parents need to be contacted to come and get them. Then I just (44)...................... them until the parents arrive to collect them. (45)......................, that's what I do.

Yesterday, however, a child came in looking a bit (46)................... . He wasn't being very clear about what was wrong with him. My colleague, who is new, actually got a bit frustrated with him and wanted to (47)....................... and send him back to class because he couldn't tell us what hurt. She's a bit of a (48).................... , and acts more like an executive manager than a nurse! I'm not at all sure she's right for the job; but back to the story. One moment he was standing there talking to us, and the next moment he was (49).............. ! He just collapsed! It still (50)............................ to think how quickly it all happened! We were working (51)........................ and we didn't even realize it at the time! Anyway, at least I (52)...................... ; we both did. We called an ambulance. It arrived in no time and the paramedics were really great; (53)............................ , professional, and they knew what they were doing. I must say, I've dealt with quite a few paramedics and they were the best ever, absolutely (54)............................ . Luckily, they tested his blood sugar right away and it was really very high. He actually had undiagnosed diabetes and was going into a coma! They gave him some insulin, and, to the boy's credit, he overcame the challenge of his sickness (55).......................... . He will have a bit of a (56)..................... though because he's going to have to take insulin for the rest of his life; from now on, insulin will be a (57)....................... for him. But at least he didn't (58)..................... !

When his parents arrived they thanked us over and over, and that really (59)....................., knowing I had made a difference in their lives. (60)......................, I think I have a very rewarding job.

Idioms Index

a bee in your bonnet: unit 2
a bird in the hand is worth two in the bush: unit 3
a blessing in disguise: unit 3
a breath of fresh air: unit 4
a dog's life: unit 9
a drop in the ocean: unit 9
a far cry from: unit 8
a necessary evil: unit 10
act your age: unit 1
add colour to something: unit 6
against the clock: unit 6
alive and kicking: unit 1
all ears: unit 9
all things considered: unit 7
allow the dust to settle: unit 9
an eye for something: unit 10
at a loose end: unit 10
at someone's beck and call: unit 2

be on the ball: unit 1
beat about/around the bush: unit 4
beggars can't be choosers: unit 2
beginner's luck: unit 2
below the belt: unit 2
better late than never: unit 2
better safe than sorry: unit 2
bite the dust: unit 9
bits and pieces: unit 3
break even: unit 4
by the book: unit 3

call it a day: unit 8
cash in your chips: unit 6
catch someone in the act: unit 1
catch someone red-handed: unit 5
catch your breath: unit 4
come in from the cold: unit 6
cook the books: unit 3
cool as a cucumber: unit 7
cost an arm and a leg: unit 1
couch potato: unit 7
count me in: unit 7
crocodile tears: unit 7
curiosity killed the cat: unit 8
curtains for someone: unit 8
cut a deal with someone: unit 9
cut it out: unit 8
cut someone dead: unit 8

day in day out: unit 8
drop dead: unit 9

early bird: unit 3
every cloud has a silver lining: unit 6

for better or worse: unit 3
from the bottom of your heart: unit 4
funny business: unit 4

get even: unit 10
get off someone's back: unit 1
get out of bed on the wrong side: unit 2
get the blues: unit 3
get to the bottom of: unit 4
get your act together: unit 1
give me a break: unit 4
give someone the creeps: unit 7
give the benefit of the doubt: unit 2
go broke: unit 4
go easy on someone: unit 10
go in one ear and out the other: unit 9
go like hot cakes: unit 5

hard cheese: unit 6
have a cross to bear: unit 8
have a crush on someone: unit 8
have all the cards: unit 5
have an ace up your sleeve: unit 1
have butterflies: unit 5
have seen better days: unit 9
have your cake and eat it: unit 5
hold in contempt: unit 7

in a class of your own: unit 6
in the blink of an eye: unit 3
into thin air: unit 1

just round the corner: unit 7

keep an eye on: unit 10
keep your cool: unit 7
kick the bucket: unit 4
kill two birds with one stone: unit 3
know no bounds: unit 4

lay your cards on the table: unit 5
let the cat out of the bag: unit 5
like chalk and cheese: unit 5
look daggers: unit 8

make a big deal of something: unit 9
make someone's day: unit 8
mind your own business: unit 5

no bed of roses: unit 2
not your cup of tea: unit 8

off colour: unit 6
once bitten, twice shy: unit 3
out cold: unit 6
out of bounds: unit 4

play cat and mouse with someone: unit 5
put all your eggs in one basket: unit 10

rings a bell: unit 2
rock the boat: unit 3

saved by the bell: unit 2
seize the day: unit 9
stab someone in the back: unit 1

take it easy: unit 10
the ball is in somebody's court: unit 1
those were the days: unit 9
to no avail: unit 1
too many cooks spoil the broth: unit 7
tough cookie: unit 7
turn a blind eye: unit 10
two in the bush: unit 3
two's company, three's a crowd: unit 6

under a cloud: unit 6
under the counter: unit 7
up to your ears: unit 10

what's the catch: unit 5
when the cat's away the mice will play: unit 5
with flying colours: unit 6

you can't teach an old dog new tricks: unit 10

your own worst enemy: unit 10

Irregular Verbs Index

Base Form	Simple Past	Past Participle
awake	awoke	awoken
be	was, were	been
bear	bore	born
beat	beat	beaten
become	became	become
begin	began	begun
bend	bent	bent
beset	beset	beset
bet	bet	bet
bid	bid/bade	bid/bidden
bind	bound	bound
bite	bit	bitten
bleed	bled	bled
blow	blew	blown
break	broke	broken
breed	bred	bred
bring	brought	brought
broadcast	broadcast	broadcast
build	built	built
burn	burned/burnt	burned/burnt
burst	burst	burst
buy	bought	bought
cast	cast	cast
catch	caught	caught
choose	chose	chosen
cling	clung	clung
come	came	come
cost	cost	cost
creep	crept	crept
cut	cut	cut
deal	dealt	dealt
dig	dug	dug
dive	dived/dove	dived
do	did	done
draw	drew	drawn
dream	dreamed/dreamt	dreamed/dreamt
drive	drove	driven
drink	drank	drunk
eat	ate	eaten
fall	fell	fallen
feed	fed	fed
feel	felt	felt
fight	fought	fought
find	found	found
fit	fit	fit
flee	fled	fled
fling	flung	flung
fly	flew	flown
forbid	forbade	forbidden
forget	forgot	forgotten
forego (forgo)	forewent	foregone
forgive	forgave	forgiven
forsake	forsook	forsaken
freeze	froze	frozen
get	got	got/gotten
give	gave	given
go	went	gone
grind	ground	ground
grow	grew	grown
hang	hung	hung
hear	heard	heard
hide	hid	hidden
hit	hit	hit
hold	held	held
hurt	hurt	hurt
keep	kept	kept
kneel	knelt	knelt
knit	knit	knit
know	knew	known
lay	laid	laid
lead	led	led
leap	leaped/leapt	leaped/leapt

Irregular Verbs Index

Base Form	Simple Past	Past Participle
learn	learned/learnt	learned/learnt
leave	left	left
lend	lent	lent
let	let	let
lie	lay	lain
light	lighted/lit	lighted/lit
lose	lost	lost
make	made	made
mean	meant	meant
meet	met	met
misspell	misspelled/misspelt	misspelled/misspelt
mistake	mistook	mistaken
mow	mowed	mowed/mown
overcome	overcame	overcome
overdo	overdid	overdone
overtake	overtook	overtaken
overthrow	overthrew	overthrown
pay	paid	paid
plead	pled	pled
prove	proved	proved/proven
put	put	put
quit	quit	quit
read	read	read
rid	rid	rid
ride	rode	ridden
ring	rang	rung
rise	rose	risen
run	ran	run
saw	sawed	sawed/sawn
say	said	said
see	saw	seen
seek	sought	sought
sell	sold	sold
send	sent	sent
set	set	set
sew	sewed	sewed/sewn
shake	shook	shaken
shave	shaved	shaved/shaven
shear	shore	shorn
shed	shed	shed
shine	shone	shone
shoe	shoed	shoed/shod
shoot	shot	shot
show	showed	showed/shown
shrink	shrank	shrunk
shut	shut	shut
sing	sang	sung
sink	sank	sunk
sit	sat	sat
sleep	slept	slept
slay	slew	slain
slide	slid	slid
sling	slung	slung
slit	slit	slit
smite	smote	smitten
sow	sowed	sowed/sown
speak	spoke	spoken
speed	sped	sped
spend	spent	spent
spill	spilled/spilt	spilled/spilt
spin	spun	spun
spit	spit/spat	spit
split	split	split
spread	spread	spread
spring	sprang/sprung	sprung
stand	stood	stood
steal	stole	stolen
stick	stuck	stuck
sting	stung	stung

Irregular Verbs

Base Form	Simple Past	Past Participle
stink	stank	stunk
stride	strode	stridden
strike	struck	struck
string	strung	strung
strive	strove	striven
swear	swore	sworn
sweep	swept	swept
swell	swelled	swelled/swollen
swim	swam	swum
swing	swung	swung
take	took	taken
teach	taught	taught
tear	tore	torn
tell	told	told
think	thought	thought
thrive	thrived/throve	thrived
throw	threw	thrown
thrust	thrust	thrust
tread	trod	trodden
understand	understood	understood
uphold	upheld	upheld
upset	upset	upset
wake	woke	woken
wear	wore	worn
weave	weaved/wove	weaved/woven
wed	wed	wed
weep	wept	wept
wind	wound	wound
win	won	won
withhold	withheld	withheld
withstand	withstood	withstood
wring	wrung	wrung
write	wrote	written